Gary Jones

# Europe Travel Guide 4

*Madrid,Barcelona,Lisbon*

# Contents

# 1

# MADRID INTRODUCTION

What comes to mind at the thought or mention of Madrid? Well, different things will probably cross different people's minds but one of the common ones will be Real Madrid Football Club, the fun people and Spanish bullfighting just to mention a few but there is more to Madrid than just that.

With a city population of over 3.3 million and a metro area that prides in over 6.5million residents coupled with the fact that it prides in its artistic and cultural heritage and a people that never sleeps, you can bet that there is a lot you can experience. Madrid is the largest city in Spain and dates back to the 2nd century BC when the Roman Empire established a settlement at the banks of Manzanares River then named it Matrice.

Over the years, the city has grown to become the headquarters of World Trade Organization (WTO), the residence of the Spanish Monarch, the seat of the government of Spain and the economic, political, and cultural center of Spain. Its urban agglomeration has the EU's third largest GDP and has been ranked the world's 17th most livable city in the world by Monocle magazine in its 2014 index.

Besides Real Madrid FC, Atlético de Madrid is also another football club with base in Madrid. Currently, Madrid has 21 districts, which have been further divided into 128 wards (also known as barrios)–the picture below shows the 21 districts. If you are planning to visit Madrid, make this book your guide as it will help you uncover many of the places you'd probably not want to miss.

I hope you enjoy your trip!

# 2

# Weather And The Best Time To Visit

The best time of the year to travel to Madrid is probably Spring and Autumn. The air is crisp and the weather mild, but the two seasons feature some differences that you may want to account for when planning a trip to the city.

Spring runs from March to May, and days are warm, while the nights are cool. People flood into the streets for the trendy "marcha" where people walk across the city, step into bars, chat on the streets, and simply have fun outdoors. Holy Week is a particularly good time to visit the city, when the residents leave the city for vacation. There are some wind and some rain, but it is generally okay.

Autumn, which runs from September, all through November, is the time schools are opened, and people get back to work after the August holidays. This is usually marked with plenty of cultural activities. Compared to the high temperatures in August, the days are very pleasant.

During winter, which runs from December to March, the number of tourists is not so much, and it can be a good time to travel, if you don't mind some cold and some snow. Since this is a low tourist season, you will enjoy great bargains at trips and hotels around Madrid.

The feared summer that runs from June, all through August is not as bad as it is publicized. The momentum is kind in June, harsh in July and harsher in August. Nights in June are long and warm, and you can really take pleasure in the party atmosphere in the streets. July is marked with temperatures hitting over 40 Degrees Celsius, and does not cool down that much during the night.

# 3

# Background And History

Madrid, originally known as Mayrit, was established at the end of the 9th century by the emir Muhammad. The city gained relevance under the Arab inhabitation of the Iberian Peninsula, given that Toledo had been the major city in the Spanish plain.

During the Christian re-conquest of Spain, Madrid changed hands from Muslims to Christians several times, leading to the mixture of cultures that features the city to date. The current location of Madrid, at the heart of Spain, was founded in 1083 by King Alfonso I. Under Christian rule, all Muslim symbols were eliminated from the city and part of the city's cultural heritage was lost.

In the course of the next centuries, Madrid developed to reach its current aspect. Plaza Mayor (The Main Square) was founded in the 13th century under the auspice of John II. Enrique III later ordered the building of El Pardo into a dwelling place for royal visits. Madrid kept growing in size, and the Spanish Court was finally transferred to the city from its current location in Toledo. It was moved again in 1601 to Valladolid, before being definitively returned to Madrid five years later.

The nineteenth century was a gloomy time for Madrid, following bloody historical events like the rise of the city against French dominance on 2nd May 1808, as well as the onset of the Spanish War of Independence.

After the death of General Franco in the 20th century, the 1978 Spanish Constitution affirmed Madrid as Spain's capital city.

The first democratic elections were held in 1979 in the city to elect the first city mayor. Enrique Tierno Galvan was voted the first governor of Madrid. By this time, the city had grown in size and population to reach a figure of three million people in the metropolitan area, and almost six million inhabitants in the entire province of Madrid.

# 4

# Transport In Madrid

### Getting In

Before you can start moving around the city, you need to get to it first. Let's take a quick look at the transport options on how to get into Madrid.

### By Plane

Adolfo Suárez Madrid-Barajas Airport (IATA: MAD, is the main international airport, and one of the largest in Europe. It is located about 13km from the city center.

Adolfo Suárez Madrid-Barajas Airport Website
http://www.aeropuertomadrid-barajas.com/eng/
Adolfo Suárez Madrid-Barajas Airport MAP
https://goo.gl/maps/NeFVg8nZYyG2
Phone:+34 913 21 10 00

When you get here, you can use the express bus services usually available 24 hours and passes all the 4 terminals then goes to O'Donell, Cibeles, which is around a 20 minutes walk or a pretty fast metro ride to Puera del Sol and Atocha. You will incur about €5, paid to the driver; there is a bus after 12 minutes during the day and every 35minutes during the night.

If you don't want to use the bus, use the metro (this is line 8pink starting from 06.30 to 01.30) to Nuevos Ministerios station. Please note that you will change the line twice if you use this option.

You can also use the public bus 200, which moves from the airport to Avenida de America bus station in Madrid. This will cost about 1.5 Euros.

If you arrive at night, use bus N4, which goes from Plaza Cibeles to Barajas district.

**By Bus**

Madrid has 8 large intercity and international bus stations. Check the tourist office for info about their destinations. If you are from Barcelona or Bilbao, you can check out buses at Avenida de America bus terminal. Other intercity buses arrive and depart from Estación Sur de Autobuses.

Bus Website

http://www.eurolines.es/en/

## By Train

You can use Renfe to and from Madrid: This will get you to either of the two main stations, Atocha and Chamartín both of which have excellent metro connections.

Train Website

http://www.eurail.com/

## By Car

If you prefer car travel, you can hire one from such global car rental car companies like Avis, Hertz, Europcar, Budget, and Thrifty.

## Moving Around Madrid

Madrid has an excellent public transport system, which is highly recommended. Nonetheless, you can move around the city using five main ways.

## Metro (Tube, subway or underground)

The trains work from 06:00 to 01:30. During the day, you won't have to wait for more than five minutes for a train. The trains become slightly scarce from around 19:00, but even then, you won't have to wait for more than thirty minutes.

The metro is a safe, clean and efficient service that's easy to navigate. It has spacious and air conditioned coaches, and many are designed with reserved seating for the disabled and the elderly. The metro is also cheap, with a single ticket going for as little as €1.50. The cheapest alternative is to purchase a ten-journey metro-bus ticket, which costs €12.20 and is applicable on the bus.

Metro Website
https://www.metromadrid.es/en
Phone:902 444 403

## Metro & public transport tickets

You can purchase an individual ticket for €1.50 to go anywhere on the metro. This is valid for a single journey on every day of the week, which passes through any zone on the network, and entitles you to an EMT bus journey as well. Metro tickets can be purchased at the automatic ticket machine or the ticket office. The tickets are priced at €1.50 for a single trip anywhere within zone A.

Metro Tickets Website
https://www.metromadrid.es/en/
viaja_en_metro/index.html
Madrid Card Website
http://www.madridcard.com/en/inicio


Note: Madrid's public transport system can be pretty complicated for a foreigner to understand. This is especially because how much you pay will ultimately depend on the line you will use, the specific number of stations, which you want to travel and the specific company that owns that line. Nonetheless, you can get more info about real time public transport system in Madrid by visiting Plan A Metro Madrid to help you understand how public transport works and the different routes. You can also get more from Madrid Tourist Guide to unleash some interesting ideas on how to move around Madrid and end up saving.


### Taxi service
Official taxis in Madrid are white with a red stripe.

*Tele taxi: +34 63 090 7990/ +34 91 371 3711/
+34 91 371 2131
*Radio taxi: +34 91 405 5500/ +34 91 405 1213/
+34 91 447 3232/ +34 91 447 5180


You can hire a taxi at night when the metro isn't running, especially if you are not familiar with your surroundings. You can either stop the taxi in the street, or wait for one at a taxi rank. The taxi ranks are shown by a blue sign, containing a white letter T. A green light will be displayed by the available taxis. You will be charged €2.05 for setting the meter, and 98 cents per kilometre after that between 06:00 and 22:00 in the city centre.

If you pick up the cab at Madrid Barajas airport, you will pay an automatic supplement of €5.50. Any trip starting from a taxi rank at railway station, approach road or bus station to either will cost a supplement charge of €2.95. This supplement is mandatory if you take your cab from a taxi zone indicating the sign "supplemento autorizado", which is displayed on a tablet at the taxi rank, reminiscent of a road sign.

## Public buses

This is another cheap, clean and efficient means of transport in Madrid, Spain. You can purchase a ten journey Metro-bus ticket for a mere €12.20, which is useable both on the bus and the metro. The EMT buses are painted red, and operate from 06:00 to 23:30. As soon as you get on the bus, simply punch your ticket into the machine. There is a bus service that operates during the night, but if you are not too familiar with your destination, it is advisable to stick to taxis for night travel.

## Terminals

*Estación Sur de Madrid: Méndez Álvaro, 83 ;
tel : +34 91 468 4200
Estacion Bus Terminal Map
https://goo.gl/maps/7HuFPHbzPro

*Alsa: Buses travel to all parts of Spain.
Tel: +34 91 327 0540
Alsa Bus Terminal Map
https://goo.gl/maps/uNpdBbmqZJk

*Socibus: Services operate to Jerez de la Frontera,
Huelva, Córodoba, Cádiz and Sevilla.
Tel: +34 90 222 9292
Socibus Map

https://goo.gl/maps/beyzz5CRGX72

*Estación de Avenida de América :
Avda. de América, 9 ; Tel : +34 90 230 2010
Estación de Avenida de América Map
https://goo.gl/maps/MzWU4suBeQD2

## Travelling within the city on a bus

The buses within the city are red, and are known as EMT, short for
Empresa Municipal de Transporte. You can use them to get to any part
of the city. They mainly operate on their own bus lanes, helping them
avoid traffic most of the time. They operate more or less between
06:00 – 23:30, in relation to the particular line. There are also night
buses that run between 23:30 and 05:00, exact times depending on
the line. The red bus stops are vividly conspicuous, with each having
a timetable attached to it.

The buses at night are referred to as "buhos", meaning "owls". You
can usually wait up to half an hour for a bus in the night, but the fare
remains the same as during the day.

These buses operate along twenty different routes, and each one
must passes through Plaza de la Cibeles. This is especially handy
because it is only fifteen minutes away from Sol and Gran Via (the
centre), where most of the nightlife is.

A single bus ticket costs €1.50, but if you plan to travel around the
city, the best value is probably to purchase a Metro-bus ticket for
€12.20 that allows you ten trips on the bus or metro.

## Walking around

Madrid's main centre is not really that big, and it's relatively safe to
walk around. Majority of the points of interest are indicated on brown
pedestrian signs depicting a walking man. If it is not too hot, it can

be nice to walk around the city in order to get your bearings better, and capture some beautiful sights along the way.

# 5

# Hotels

## Accommodation

There are several types of accommodation in Madrid, with each catering for different types of needs. Hotels are ideal for business people or couples, apartments offer great value and facilities for groups, families or anyone who wants to feel like they are truly experiencing the city. On the other hand, a hostal, which is more like a guesthouse, provides quality accommodation while a youth hostel is ideal for backpackers or anyone on a tight budget.

### Budget hotels

These hotels all have 2 stars. You will be charged roughly €60.00 for a twin room.

· **\*Asturias**

Tel: +34 91 429 6676

(Calle Sevilla, 2, 28014 Madrid)

This hotel has one hundred and seventy five rooms. It is a central location with clubs, bars, and shops nearby.

Asturias Hotel Website

http://www.hotel-asturias.com/

Asturias Map

https://goo.gl/maps/QL7JjyoppgN2

· **\*Mediodia**

Tel: +34 91 527 3060
(Plaza Emperador Carlos V, 8, 28012 Madrid)
This is a big hotel with one hundred and seventy three rooms, and it is close to the Atocha train station and the Reina Sofia Museum.
Mediodia Hotel Website
http://www.mediodiahotel.com/en/
Mediodia Hotel Map
https://goo.gl/maps/sr6848e3qmv

• *Mora

Tel: +34 91 420 1569
(Paseo del Prado, 32, 28014 Madrid)
This hotel has sixty-two rooms, with a convenient distance from Atocha train station, as well as a walking distance to the Reina Sofia Museum.
Mora Hotel Website
http://www.hotelmora.com/index.php/en
Mora Hotel Map
https://goo.gl/maps/PsD8jvQWJ1M2

• *Santander

Tel: +34 91 429 9551
(Calle Echegaray, 1, 28014 Madrid)
This hotel has thirty-five rooms, and is in a central location.
Santander Hotel Website
http://casualhoteles.com/hoteles-madrid/casual-del-teatro/
Santander Hotel Map
https://goo.gl/maps/R61bZKB5dpL2

**Hostals**

This is similar to a hotel in style, since you pay for both a bathroom and bedroom, but it does not come with the same facilities. It is therefore cheaper than a hotel. You can rent a room with its own bathroom, or one with a shared bathroom. There will be towels and television available, but many do not offer breakfast. Generally, hostels are designed in a modern style and are clean and pleasant places to stay.

- **\*Hostal Astoria**

Tel: +34 91 429 1188
  (Carrera de San Jerónimo 30–32, 28014 Madrid)
  Hostal Astoria Website
  http://www.hostal-astoria.com/en/
  Hostal Astoria Map
  https://goo.gl/maps/2Mxs8NkYUxm
- **\*Ostal Gran Duque**

Tel: +34 91 540 0413
  (Calle Campomanes, 6 – 3º, 28013 Madrid)
  Ostal Gran Duque Website
  http://en.granhotelcondeduque.com/
  Ostal Gran Duque Map
  https://goo.gl/maps/GvrTiBdjQM62
- **\*Hostal Don Diego**

Tel: +34 91 521 1339
  (Calle Velazquez, 45, 28001 Madrid)
  Hostal Don Diego Website
  http://www.hostaldondiego.com/en/
  Hostal Don Diego Map
  https://goo.gl/maps/4JzqCttvuBm

**Youth hostels**

Do not confuse between a hostal and a youth hostel. A youth hostel, or Albergue Juvenile, has shared sleeping dormitories (typically of the same sex), and sometimes a few group or family rooms for rent. They are one of the most cost effective means of accommodation, and a bed will cost you roughly €15.00 per night. They are a great place to meet other students and travelers, and you will be able to access loads of information from other residents about what is happening in the city.

REAJ, the Youth hostels Network, is responsible for the IYHF in Spain.

- **\*REAJ**

Tel: +34 91 720 1165
Youth Hostels Website
https://www.hihostels.com/

# 6

# Museums

Madrid has more than forty-four museums. Here are a few of the most popular:

- **\*The Royal Palace**

Tel: +34 91 454 8800; Street: Bailen

Opened from 10:30 to 6:00pm (Monday to Saturday, October to March); 10:00am to 6:00pm (Sundays and holidays); and 10:00am to 8:00pm (Monday to Sunday, including holidays, April to September)

Entry fee: 10 Euros without a guide; 17 Euros with a guide. Free access for children under five, and 5Euros for pre-arranged visit

This is one of the most visited museums in the city. It was built during the Bourbon reign between the seventeenth and eighteenth centuries. Although the Spanish Royal Family no longer lives here, they still use it for state events. The porcelain room is one of the more unusual rooms, where the walls are covered with white and green porcelain.

Royal Palace Website
http://www.patrimonionacional.es/en
Royal Palace Map
https://goo.gl/maps/KeHJ54CUeJr

- **\*Lazaro Galdiano Museum**

Tel: +34 91 561 6084; Street: C/ Serrano, 122
Opened from 10:00am to 4:30pm (Wednesday to Monday)
Entry fee: 4 Euros; free on Wednesdays

This museum was originally Jose Lazaro Galdiano's house, who was a financier, editor and writer. He lived between 1862 and 1947, during which time he established an extensive art collection, along several unusual items.

Lazaro Galdiano Website
http://www.flg.es/
Lazaro Galdiano Map
https://goo.gl/maps/qBVmyksEFSr
- **\*The Museum of America**

Tel: +34 91 549 2641; Street: Avda. Reyes Catolicos, 6

Opened from 9:30am to 8:30pm Tuesday to Saturday (1st May to 31st October); 9:30am to 6:30pm Tuesday to Saturday (1st November to 30th April); and 10:00am to 3:00pm (Sundays and public holidays)

Entry fee: 3 Euros; free for over 65s and under 18s.

This interesting museum is filled with artifacts from Spain's colonization of the Americas. It covers over two floors, with many pieces preserved since prehistoric times. Here, you will find gold ornaments from Columbia and Mayan parchments from AD 1250.

Museum of America Website
http://www.mecd.gob.es/museodeamerica/
en/el-museo.html
Museum of America Map
https://goo.gl/maps/zFazYbakqb62

- **\*Traje Museum**

Tel: +34 91 550 4700
Opened from 9:30am to 7:00pm Tuesday to Saturday; 10:00am to 3:00pm Sundays and Public holidays.

Entry fee: 3 Euros; Free entry with a Madrid Card; as well as Sundays, Saturday afternoons, World Heritage Day (18 April), International Museum Day (18 May), National Fiesta of Spain (12 October) and Constitution Day (6 December)

This museum is all about Spanish clothing from the eighteenth, nineteenth, and twentieth centuries. The rooms house clothing from different eras, as well as temporary exhibitions.

Traje Museum Website
http://museodeltraje.mcu.es/index.jsp?lang=eng
Traje Museum Map
https://goo.gl/maps/VD4A4yav37v
- **\*Naval Museum**

Tel: +34 91 523 8789; Street: Paseo del Prado, 5
Opened from 10:00am to 6:00pm (Tuesday to Sunday);
Closed from 19th July to 1st September (summer).
Entry: free

Here you will find replicas of the Spanish Navy arsenal from the eighteenth century. The history of the navy is illustrated through charts, weapons, and paintings. Each room shows a different period in history, starting with the fifteenth century to the present day.

Naval Museum Website
http://www.armada.mde.es/ArmadaPortal/page/

Portal/ArmadaEspannola/ciencia_museo/prefLang_en/
Naval Museum Map
https://goo.gl/maps/LaJ7uZcNocF2
· **\*Real Madrid Stadium**

Tel: +34 91 453 2902; St: Pº de la Castellana, 144,
Estadio Santiago Bernabéu, Puerta 3
Opened from 10:00am to 7:30pm Monday to Saturday (Days with no matches); and 10:30am to 6:30pm Sundays
Entry fee: Under fourteen – 11 Euros; Adults – 16 Euros

You can visit the Real Madrid Museum when touring the stadium. The museum is broad and full of trophies that date back over the entire history of the teams. In addition, there is a wall of photographs of all the Real Madrid Players to have ever existed, as well as autographed boots and shirts from the first team.

Real Madrid Stadium Website
http://www.realmadrid.com/en/santiago-bernabeu-stadium
Real Madrid Stadium Map
https://goo.gl/maps/eowdGVACPGN2

**Extra Time In Madrid**
Other notable museums worth visiting include:
· **Museum Cerralbo**

Museum Cerralbo Website
http://en.museocerralbo.mcu.es/
Museum Cerralbo Map
https://goo.gl/maps/FmRWa2rJk5B2
· **National Archaeological Museum of Spain**

National Archaeological Website
http://www.man.es/man/en/home
National Archaeological Map
https://goo.gl/maps/5C3dohU34uR2

# 7

# Art Galleries

- <u>*The Prado</u>

Prado Art Gallery, Tel: +34 91 330 2800; Street: Paseo Del Prado
  Opened from Tuesday to Sunday (9:00am to 8:00pm)
  €12.00 entry fee; free entry for official guides, teachers, disabled,
unemployed EU students below age 25, and over 65s

This is probably the most famous art gallery in Madrid. It accommodates a wide collection of works from the twelfth to the nineteenth centuries. Here, you will see some of the most talked about paintings in the world, including works by Murillo, Rubens, and Goya.

Prado Website
https://www.museodelprado.es/en/
Prado Map
https://goo.gl/maps/uPk4h7zDXWJ2
· **<u>*Reina Sofia</u>**

Reina Sofia Art Gallery; Tel: +34 91 774 1000; street: Santa Isabel, 52
Opened from 10:00am to 9:00pm (Monday to Saturday), and 10:00am to 2:30pm on Sundays.

Entry fee: 6 Euros; free for the general public from 2:30pm to 9:30pm

Saturdays, 10:00am to 2:30pm Sundays, and on 6th December, 12th October and 18th May.

This is an impressive art gallery where you can see relatively recent works from the twentieth and twenty-first centuries. There are several Picasso pieces, including the popular Guernica, and a separate section designated for some modern art sculptures, as well as a room showing a film written by Salvador Dali and Bunuel.

Reina Sofia Website
http://www.museoreinasofia.es/en
Reina Sofia Map
https://goo.gl/maps/Dk7DHHhb6V62
· **\*Thyssen Bornemisza**

Thyssen Bornemisza Art Gallery; Tel: +34 91 369 0151; Street: Paseo del Prado, 8
  Open from 10:00am to 7:00pm (Tuesday to Sunday)
  Entry fee: 8 Euros for adults; 5:50 Euros for students and pensioners; free for children under twelve (accompanied)

This is one of the most popular art galleries, and the main building is known as Villahermosa Palace. The paintings here are said to be among the best private collections from the thirteenth to the twentieth century art. Here, you will see Rothko, Kandinsky, Renoir, Degas, Goya, Titian or Durero. There are guided tours for families with children aged between six and twelve years at the weekends. You must call to book in advance.

Thyssen Bornemisza Website
http://www.museothyssen.org/en/thyssen/home
Thyssen Bornemisza Map
https://goo.gl/maps/gPRVwPUcrg32

- **\*Sorolla Art Gallery**

Tel: +34 91 310 1584; Street: del General Martínez Campos, 37
   Opened from 9:30 am to 8:00pm (Tuesday to Saturday); and 10:00am to 3:00pm (Sundays and public holidays)
   Entry fee: 3 Euros for Adults; free for pensioners and students, and on Sundays.

This is a less publicized museum, but one of the little known treasures in Madrid. The art gallery was originally inhabited by Joaquin Sorolla y Bastida, the Valencian artist. It was built from 1910 to 1911. Here, you will find excellent ceramic works and sculptures, as well as jewelry and furniture.

Sorolla Website
http://museosorolla.mcu.es/
Sorolla Map
https://goo.gl/maps/tWEXD46bof62

# 8

# Shopping In Madrid

Shopping in Madrid is so much fun because there are very many different styles to select from. The prices are fairly reasonable, unless you are shopping in designer boutiques.

There are 5 areas you should head off too if you are looking to shop in Madrid: Cuatro Caminos, Princesa, Chueca and Salamanca. Each area serves different budgets and tastes.

Chueca is a popular bohemian area where you can find designer and original goods, with price tags to match. Calle Hortaleza is one of the best streets to visit. Chueca is particularly good for shoe shopping. It's not far from the center, and you can walk to the area in five minutes if you are in Gran Via.

Chueca Map
https://goo.gl/maps/rUW5AfjyDdK2

Shopping in the center of the city is a delight. The most obvious areas to visit are the Puerta del Sol, Gran Via, Plaza Mayor and the nearby streets. You will find Spanish high street names such as El Corte Ingles, Fnac, Bershka, Pimkie and Zara.

Puerta del Sol Map
https://goo.gl/maps/G9tyXVdfK8N2
Gran Via Map
https://goo.gl/maps/YLTKXDzcAx32
Plaza Mayor Map
https://goo.gl/maps/51i1YC7SNAS2

If you are working on a budget, consider shopping close to the university in Arguelles. Begin your shopping on the streets of Alberto Aguilera and Princesa. Cuatro Caminos, located in the north of the city, is another great bargain paradise. It is located between the streets of Orense and Bravo Murillo, close to Plaza de Castilla.

Arguelles Map
https://goo.gl/maps/JUnvt3MG4Ww
Cuatro Caminos Map
https://goo.gl/maps/aNYL4co5yjt

# 9

# Dining In Madrid

## Dining In Madrid

Madrid has the richest variety of cuisine in Spain. Its public eating spots cover everything, including Andalusian gazpacho, Valencian paella, Galician pulpo (octopus), Basque bacalao (cod), and Asturian fabada (strong pork stew). You will also find Madrid's very own lamb and vegetable stew (cocido), tripe (callos), and the lesser popular oreja (ears).

The dishes in the region are both logical and hearty, given the winter climate and setting, but the most interesting thing is that the city is actually landlocked. It is surrounded by a large arid plateau, and receives a daily fish supply that is transported through large containers from the Atlantic north to supply top restaurants such as Cabo Mayor and La Trainera, with the best and freshest seafood in the country.

#### Meals

*Breakfast:  Breakfast is typically tea, hot chocolate or coffee, with assorted rolls, jam and butter.  Spanish breakfast might also include churros, which are thin, fried doughnuts, or porras (which are basically bigger churros).

*Lunch: This is the most important meal of the day in the country, and is reminiscent to the midday, farm style dinner in the U.S. It usually includes 3 or 4 courses, starting with an option of soup or a variety of dishes of hors d'oeuvres known as entremeses. Usually, a dish of egg or fish is served after this, followed by a meat dish with vegetables. Wine is always included in the meal. Dessert is typically assorted fruit, custard, or pastry, followed by coffee. Lunchtime starts from 1:00 to 4:00 pm, with rush hour being at 2:00 pm.

*Tapas: Once they are done with their early evening strolls, most Spaniards head to their favourite bars, tascas where they drink wine and bite assorted tapas (snacks), like olives, eggs in mayonnaise, or bits of fish.

Since most Spaniards take their dinner very late, they usually eat an extremely light breakfast, mostly coffee and maybe a pastry. But they often get hungry by 11:00 am, and since lunch might not be ready until 1:00 pm, they usually take a late morning snack at a cafeteria. Most preferred items to order include an empanada (slice of fish or meat pie from Galicia) or tortilla (omelette with potatoes) accompanied with a caña of beer or a copa of wine. Enquire for a doble if you want a larger beer. Many people ask for a large tapa, like squid (calamares), or tripe (callos), also served with wine or beer and bread.

*Dinner: A typical meal begins with a bowl of soup, with the second course usually being a fish dish, and a third main course, usually pork, beef, or veal, served with vegetables. Again, desserts are often pastries, custard, or fruit.

If you had a late and heavy lunch and stopped at a tapas bar before dinner, supper will automatically be much lighter, perhaps a bowl of soup, sausage, some cold cuts, or a Spanish omelet with potatoes. Wine is always included in the meal. Typically, dining usually begins at 10:00 or 10:30pm.

### Where to eat
· **Alkalde**

Address: Calle de Jorge Juan, 10, Madrid
Phone: +34 915 76 33 59
Alkalde Website
http://www.alkalderestaurante.com/
Alkalde Map
https://goo.gl/maps/WFUwfE7btYD2
· **Bazaar Restaurant**

Address: Calle de la Libertad, 21, Madrid
Phone: +34 915 23 39 05
Bazaar Website

http://www.grupandilana.com/es/restaurantes/bazaar
Bazaar Map
https://goo.gl/maps/oScyUCWuFG32

· **Sobrino de Botin**

This is the world oldest Restaurant; they serve traditional Spanish food from different regions.

Address: Calle Cuchilleros, 17, 28005 Madrid
Phone: +34 913 66 42 17
Sobrino de Botin Website
http://www.botin.es/?q=en
Sobrino de Botin Map
https://goo.gl/maps/xu31t8TD6tv

· **Ribeira do Mino**

Try some amazing Galician seafood Ribeira do Mino.

Address: Calle de Sta Brigida, 1, Madrid
Phone: +34 915 21 98 54
Ribeira do Mino Website
http://www.marisqueriaribeiradomino.com/
en/des-752-home
Ribeira do Mino Map
https://goo.gl/maps/ATeDHDJ1BNs

· **Paella de la Reina**

Eat some of the best Valencian paella at Paella de la Reina.

Address: Calle de la Reina, 39, 28004 Madrid
Phone: +34 915 31 18 85
Paella de la Reina
http://www.lapaelladelareina.com/
Paella de la Reina
https://goo.gl/maps/G3K5bnu9i1w

# 10

# Bars And Nightlife

Madrid loves to party. With near-compulsory siestas after lunch and sometimes in the evening as well, who can blame the three million inhabitants of this great city for wanting to burn off all the excess energy? Despite its flair and cultural sophistication, Madrid's vibrant nightlife and unpretentious bar scene provide endless opportunities to do just that. At a time when most tourists from the more sensible parts of the world might be settling into a pair of slippers and warm cocoa, Madrileños are just getting started. If you have the urge and liveliness to join them, here is a quick sample of what is on offer in Madrid after dark.

### 8:00pm: Tapas, canas and friends
Going out in Madrid usually starts with a relaxing after work drink that soon turns into a frantic adventure, rarely ending before 2:00 am. Some of the reasons behind the late schedule include the exceptionally strong cocktails, a rather laid-back attitude on when and where to meet, and the utter volume of venues from which to choose from.

However, once you have committed yourself to going out, it is probably best to give up any other plans for the evening and simply enjoy the ride. Unlike many nightlife scenes, what you wear is not particularly significant – it is not unusual to see a posh individual (a well dressed pijo) interacting with a T-shirt sporting twenty-something. The best locations to soak up the local ambiance are the areas of La Latina, Malasana and Plaza de Santa Ana, which are ever bustling, particularly at night. Most young people (and not-so-young individuals) gather at one of the many tapas bars to enjoy cold beers (canas) with an array of tapas. But be warned – many tapas bars are small and tend to get overcrowded with standing room only.
 • **\*Lateral, Paseo de La Castellana**

Open from 8:00am to 1:00am (Monday to Wednesday); 8:00am to 2:00am (Thursday and Friday); 12:00pm to 2:00 am (Saturday) and 12:00pm to 1:00 am (Sunday).

Phone: +34 914 20 15 82
Lateral Website
http://www.lateral.com/
Lateral Map
https://goo.gl/maps/8zRb8JBJLxF2

· **\*Le Cabrera, Calle de Dona Barbara de Braganza 2**

Open from 4:00pm to 2:00 am (Monday to Thursday); 4:00pm to 2:30am (Friday and Saturday); and from 1:30pm (Sunday brunch).
  Standouts include an impressive collection of cocktails starting from €11 and the foie gras topped burgers.

Phone: +34 913 19 94 57
Le Cabrera Website
http://www.cienllaves.com/terraza/
Le Cabrera Map
https://goo.gl/maps/r5CpB3fBkKG2

10:00pm – Copas
If you are not satisfied with tapas, it is good to know that 10:00 pm is the earliest time Madrileños venture out to dinner, and most restaurants account for this schedule. Some people remain at the bars and order larger raciones, while others, recuperating from their evening siestas, are rejuvenated and ready for the night's revelries. After the evening meal, it is usually time to enjoy some cocktails or copas, as opposed to wine.
· **\*Bristol Bar, Calle del Almirante 20**

Open from 10:00 am to 1:00 am (Monday to Wednesday); 10:00 am to 2:00am (Thursday and Friday); 11:00am to 2:00am (Saturday)
  During summertime, it is standard to hop from one terrace venue to the next between 2:00am and 3:00am. When it gets colder, folks

usually stay at their favorite bars until it is time to venture into the clubs. It is usually challenging to keep up with changing trends in a city as cosmopolitan as this, but locals still remain obsessed with the classic tonic and gin. Tours, tastings and entire bars are designated for the timeless combination, like the Brit-motivated Bristol Bar.

Phone: +34 915 22 45 68
Bristol Bar Website
http://bristolbar.es/
Bristol Bar Map
https://goo.gl/maps/JwENRf69g2v
- **\*Ramses, Plaza de la Independencia**

Open from 11:00am to 2:30 am every day
Interior design enthusiasts love the Philippe Starck décor at this ultra chic bar and restaurant.

Phone:+34 914 35 16 66
Ramses Website
http://www.ramseslife.com/
Ramses Map
https://goo.gl/maps/9iWfGDG1Y6o
- **\*Museo Chicote, Gran Via 12**

Open from 5:00pm to 3:00am (Sunday to Thursday); 5:00pm to 3:30am (Friday and Saturday)
If you are up for a sense of nostalgia, you might love this art deco bar that has hosted luminaries such as Hemingway, Gardner, and Sinatra since its establishment in 1931.

Phone:+34 915 32 67 37
Museo Chicote Website
http://grupomercadodelareina.com/en/museo-chicote-en/

Museo Chicote Map
https://goo.gl/maps/dbmfnA26K842

### 3:00am: Nightclubs

When the bars close up, the diehards continue partying at the many nightclubs in the city. Most are opened at midnight but only start swinging after 1:30am. For the clubs that stay open until 6:00am at the very least, things don't generally heat up until 4:00am.

- **\*Joy Eslava, Calle Arsenal 11**

Open from 11:30 pm every day

The constant factor is the collective energy that fuels the legendary nightlife of Madrid long after the majority of cities have hit the sack. The dance floor at Joy Eslava is enormous, the crowd is mixed, and the décor is slightly dated. However, with a low cover charge, inventive club nights, and surprise appearances from ostentatious dancers, it offers kitschy, harmless fun until 6:00am.

Phone:+34 913 66 54 39
Joy Eslava Website
http://joy-eslava.com/Joy_Madrid/Bienvenida.html
Joy Eslava Map
https://goo.gl/maps/n8ZPJpDJ2GJ2

- **\*Gabana 1800, Calle Velazquez 6**

Open from 12:00am to 5:00am (Wednesday to Sunday)

As you might expect, there is a VIP tables galore, a velvet rope, and an impressive list of celebrity visitors. It has a strict door policy, so hopefuls come early.

Phone:+34 915 75 18 46
Gabana Website
http://www.gabana.es/

Gabana Map

https://goo.gl/maps/VTMgFrwmWM52

# 11

# Special Things To Do While In Madrid

**<u>Eat at Botin</u>:** This is the world's oldest restaurant and has featured in the Guinness Book of Records.

Botin Website
http://www.botin.es/?q=en
Botin Map
https://goo.gl/maps/Hdr7sL2Aa8T2

**Watch Real Madrid Playing:** If you love football, Real Madrid Football Club has many of the world's best football players. Watching them play live from their home stadium, Santiago Bernabeu Stadium, will definitely be an experience you will never forget.

Real Madrid Website
http://www.realmadrid.com/en/santiago-bernabeu-stadium
Real Madrid Map
https://goo.gl/maps/fmymBPxSgqu

**Watch Flamenco:** Madrid prides in having some of the world's finest flamenco dancers.

Flamenco Website
http://www.flamencotickets.com/
madrid-flamenco-shows

**Shop at the El Rastro:** This weekly flea market has literally anything you can think of so visiting it to buy a few souvenirs won't be such a bad idea. This is the largest flea market in Europe.

Address: Calle Ribera de Curtidores
Phone:+34 915 29 82 10
El Rastro Map
https://goo.gl/maps/Qb4h4cGgdnG2

**Watch bullfighting in Ventas Bullring:** Madrid has some of the best bullfighters in Spain so schedule to attend one of the fixtures. You can learn more about bullfighting in Madrid here.

Address: Plaza del Carmen 1
Phone: +34 915 319 131
Bullfighting Website

https://www.bullfightticketsmadrid.com/en/home

**Try riding on Madrid's cable car:** Riding the famously called teleferico will definitely give you breathtaking views of Madrid as you tour different attraction sites.

Address: Paseo del Pintor Rosales
Phone: +34 902 34 50 02
Teleferico Website
http://teleferico.com/
Teleferico Map

**Try exploring Madrid's green places:**One of its very famous is Casa de Campo , which is five times bigger than New York's Central Park. You can also check out El Retiro Park where you can hire a rowboat or even check out the statute of the Fallen Angel.

Address: Paseo Puerta del Angel, 1
Casa de Campo Map
https://goo.gl/maps/fi1KMaQoBQy

Address: Plaza de la Independencia, 7
Phone: +34 915 30 00 41
El Retiro Park Map
https://goo.gl/maps/Ce7xEPboBtS2

**Try the famous chocolate con churros:** These are really tasty sticks of fried dough eaten by just dunking in a mug of warm dipping chocolate. It tastes more like the Spanish biscuits and tea.

Address: Pasadizo San Ginés, 5
Phone: +34 913 65 65 46
Con Churros Website
https://chocolateriasangines.com/
Con Churros Map
https://goo.gl/maps/UnEzGCb2hvG2

**See the spectacular city gate Puerto de Alcala:** This is especially amazing at night. It was constructed by Francesco Sabatini for King Charles III. You can learn more about it here.

Address: Plaza de la Independencia, 1
Puerto de Alcala Map
https://goo.gl/maps/tYhZnyzPCVo

**See the Golden Triangle:** This one is formed by the city's 3 main museums, Reina Sofia Museum, Thyssen Boremisza and Prado Museum.

Reina Sofia Museum Map
https://goo.gl/maps/RUayEfC4k5T2

Thyssen Boremisza Map
https://goo.gl/maps/YMkhtUhYWvS2
Prado Museum Map
https://goo.gl/maps/gwh8XjD8nHM2

**Visit the Temple of Debod:**This is definitely one of the unusual places to see in Parque del Oeste; this is a park just near the Royal Palace. You can learn more about it here.

Temple of Debod Map
https://goo.gl/maps/ogfqNQV7Krr

# 12

# Three Day Sample Itinerary

## Three Day Sample Itinerary

Madrid is an astonishingly easy city to get around, be it by public transportation or by foot. Do not stress about tipping; a few coins for meal service will usually be enough. Generally, wait-staff are not awfully attentive: If you want to ask for the bill or place an order, you can simply flag down any waiter. While the city is relatively safe, there is plenty of petty theft. Always mind your belongings because pickpockets do not discriminate against tourists.

### Day One

- **\*Royal Palace of Madrid**

This is the place to experience Spanish richness at its best. The rooms are a genuine wonderland of red velvet thrones, crystal chandeliers, and ceiling murals galore.

While you are there, visit the Almudena Cathedral in the neighborhood. Entrance is free, but a small donation is still welcomed. Plan to stay for one to two hours.

Address: Calle de Bailén, 3

Phone: +34 914 54 87 00
Royal Palace Map
https://goo.gl/maps/RWFxNaY7ViQ2
- *Plaza Mayor

Surround yourself with Madrid culture in the main square of the capital, Plaza Mayor. On summer, it floods with outdoor terrazas where tourists and locals alike drink and dine al fresco. During winter, it is covered with an array of lights that highlights the yearly Christmas fair.

Plaza Mayor houses some of the most classic gift shops, where you can acquire traditional Spanish souvenirs, including thimbles and hats. It is usually filled with street performers and real-sized cartoon characters. Plan to stay for less than an hour.

Plaza Mayor Map
https://goo.gl/maps/f6tz89J9M9s
- *Puerta del Sol

This is the most classic meeting point in the city. Many bus and metro lines pass through here, and all the radial freeways in the country are measured from a little plaque in the square. Puerta del Sol also hosts one of the biggest events of the year: New Year's Eve. The locals celebrate by quickly eating twelve grapes in a row, and in tune with the strikes of the clock.

If you are hungry, you can grab something sweet to eat at the La Mallorquina bakery, which is over a century old. Plan to stay for less than an hour.

Puerta del Sol Map
https://goo.gl/maps/3254KMhcnCw

- **\*La Latina**

Experience the best tapas hopping culture in Madrid by visiting La Latina, a tapas bar-filled neighborhood. If you happen to be in Madrid on Sunday, be sure to pass by the neighboring El Rastro outdoor market. Plan to stay for two to three hours.

La Latina Map
https://goo.gl/maps/znWJhbs7JY32

### Day Two
- **\*Gran Via**

This is the busiest street in Madrid, and arguably the most attractive thoroughfare. It is also where you can find a heavy concentration of internationally known stores and theaters. Go there to shop, see a show, or just wonder at the buzz of the big city. Plan to stay for less than an hour.

Gran Via Map
https://goo.gl/maps/jkoC78c4pVE2
- **\*Plaza de Cibeles**

There is probably no panorama more charming than the Plaza de Cibeles, with the grand Cibeles Palace and the chariot topped fountain. The H.Q. of the Spanish postal service was once based in the Cibeles Palace, but it is now home to the City Hall and a cultural center known as CentroCentro. Plan to stay for less than an hour.

Plaza de Cibeles Map
https://goo.gl/maps/CAwHnfQwGfC2

- **\*Retiro Park (Parque del Retiro)**

This is where all the city clickers in Spain go to get a dose of fresh air. Go there to row a boat, take a stroll, or sit back and enjoy a beverage at one of the several outdoor cafes. If you are a museum or art buff, and have some time to spare, visit the neighboring Prado Museum that is home to some of the finest artwork in Europe. The Glass Palace or Palacio de Cristal is free to enter and usually hosts fascinating installations and art exhibitions. Plan to stay for one to two hours.

Retiro Park Map
https://goo.gl/maps/mHW7fqWGp4C2
- **\*Barrio de Salamanca**

This neighborhood is famous for its specially posh residents, as well as the fancy restaurants and shops that they frequent. Plan to stay for one to two hours.

Barrio de Salamanca Map
https://goo.gl/maps/LuzhVfaM5892

### Day Three
- *San Anton Market

Recently renovated, this is a new hotspot for gastro lovers, especially because it is one part old fashioned, complete with fish, produce and meat stands, and the other part modern connoisseur paradise, including tapas bars and a rooftop bar & restaurant. Plan to stay for one to two hours.

Address: Calle de Augusto Figueroa, 24B
Phone: +34 913 30 07 30
San Anton Market Map
https://goo.gl/maps/afqPRqYhYAB2
- *Plaza del Dos de Mayo

This is the heart and soul of the city's diverse Malasana neighborhood, and the location of numerous outdoor terrazos, playgrounds, and often even flea markets and fairs. This is the perfect place to grab a tinto de verano or cana as you mix with the locals and just watch. In the side streets of the neighborhood, you will discover funky shops, cafes, and restaurants. Plan to stay for one to two hours.

Plaza del Dos de Mayo Map
https://goo.gl/maps/Kaq734p5XB52
- *Antigua Casa Crespo

Spanish souvenirs do not get more legit than a pair of espadrilles (alpargatas) from this family run establishment that is over a century year old. The shoes are completely Spanish made, and very affordable, with a pair going for under ten Euros. The service is also phenomenal, and the scenery will make you feel like you are going back in time. Plan to stay for less than an hour.

Address: Calle del Divino Pastor, 29
Phone: +34 915 21 56 54
Antigua Casa Crespo Website
https://www.antiguacasacrespo.com/password
Antigua Casa Crespo Map

- **\*Bodega de la Ardosa**

As far as Spanish bars are concerned, this is about as classic as it gets. Think shelves piled with dusty wine bottles, colorfully tiled walls, and memorabilia from the establishment's 100 years+ in business. The best part is their addictively tasty tortilla Espanola, notoriously considered to be one of the best in the city. Plan to stay for less than an hour.

Address: Calle de Colón, 13
Phone:+34 915 21 49 79
Bodega de la Ardosa Website
http://www.laardosa.es/
Bodega de la Ardosa Map
https://goo.gl/maps/qntravw46eu

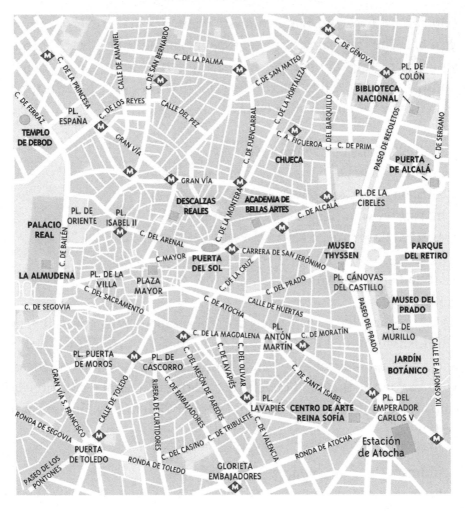

# 13

# BARCELONA INTRODUCTION

This book was created for the short stay traveler.If you have limited time in Barcelona and want to experience the best the city has to offer,then this book will help you get the most out of your short stay.

Not many cities in the world have the atmosphere, and unique experience Barcelona has to offer.You will think of this amazing city long after you leave.

You will experience unique restaurants, strange museums, amazing bars, secret gardens and amazing tours.

Barcelona is a cosmopolitan city and in this great city you will experience elegance, harmony, and good manners. You will experience a world city and share public spaces with people from around the world that call Barcelona their home.

This cosmopolitan nature of Barcelona creates something special in the heart of Spain. The city is exciting and stimulating.

Thank you for downloading my book, and I hope you have an amazing time in Barcelona!

Good Luck!

# 14

# The Quirky Side of Barcelona

It is no secret that Barcelona was placed under the world's spotlight when it hosted the Olympics in 1992. The beginnings of its rise as one of the most popular tourist destinations in the world began at that moment. There were a lot of drastic changes made because of the said event.

National Geographic called Spain's second largest city as the Best Beach City of 1992. However, before the Olympic Games, the beaches of the city were literally overrun by factories and different industries. The city government actually had to move the businesses from the seashore and convert its entire 4.5 coastline into a beach and leisure area.

In effect, this piece of coast (and the rest of the city as well) was radically changed into the stuff that tourists adore today. If you're looking for a place that combines both the quirky and cool with the seriously gothic in one cup, then Barcelona will be quite a good pick.

### What to Expect During your Visit
Many of the things you will find in and around Barcelona typically exhibit what you mostly will see in many European cities. You'll find plenty of museums, churches, restaurants, outdoor markets, shops and many historic landmarks; but those are not the only things that

make people want to come back – it's the city's cool character that usually draws in visitors in droves.

## When to Visit Barcelona?

The quick and simple answer to this question is any time of the year is a good time to visit. Of course, the summer months starting in June are the most popular. People flock to the city's beaches to enjoy and relax.

However, the city is still bustling with life even during the off peak season. Do take note that many of the shops and some places of interest are closed starting in the month of August. The shop owners also need a break and they usually make the most of the off season by going on a much deserved vacation themselves.

Nevertheless, even in the cold autumn and winter months, tourists still flock to see the historic places here. They may not go to the beach during that time of the year but they visit the place for the appreciation of art and architecture. The serious side of the city is accentuated by the cold weather and the occasional rain.

# 15

# Transportation and Safety

The best way to get from the city is to take the RENFE train from the airport.The RENFE train service runs approximately every 30 minutes to and from Barcelona airport.The train will take you to the city centre. It takes about 25 min to get to the city.You can get off at Barcelona Sants, Passeig de Gràcia or Clot Stations.At these stations, you can connect to the Subway system.

Barcelona International Airport Website
http://www.aena-aeropuertos.es/en/barcelona-airport/index.html
Barcelona International Airport Map
https://goo.gl/maps/7YiUEnuGenn
Phone:+34 902 40 47 04

RENFE Website (airport train)
http://www.renfe.com/EN/viajeros/

Metro Website
http://www.tmb.cat/en/home

The best way to get around the city is to use the subway.Barcelona
has a world-class subway system.The subway is clean, safe and easy

to use.Prices are reasonable, and various types of tickets can be purchased from vending machines.

The best ticket deal is to buy a city travel card that will give you access to the tram,metro and bus systems.This will cost around 5 euro.With these cards, you have unlimited use for the whole day.

Metro Website

http://www.tmb.cat/en/home

Travel Card Website

http://www.tmb.cat/en/barcelona-travel-card

## Safety

Barcelona is a safe city in general, however there are some problems with pickpocketing .Pickpocket criminals target tourists in places like subways or popular tourist spots.So be careful and make sure your valuables are in a safe place and not an easy target for a thief.

Be careful in the Ramblas. The Ramblas is the main promenade through the central part of the city. It is here that many pickpockets look for potential targets. So be careful. Its also a good idea to be very careful in this area at night and try to avoid it after 11pm.

These pickpockets sometimes work in teams and will try and use distractions to get you to lower your guard. So be on the lookout when strangers try to get too close to your personal space. It might be a setup to steal something from you.

It might be a good idea not to carry all your cash and credit cards in the same wallet. Leave some backup money at the hotel safe.

Have a great time in Barcelona, but be cautious!

# 16

# Hotels

### We Boutique Hotel

The building where this lovely hotel is located was once home to the famous painter Josep Maria Sert.Josep Maria Sert was a friend of Salvador Dalí, the world renowned artist.The We Boutique Hotel is very elegant, and its location is great.The hotel only has six rooms, so it's nice and cosy with great service.

Address:2a, Ronda de Sant Pere, 70, Barcelona
Phone:+34 932 50 39 91
We Boutique Hotel Website
http://www.weboutiquehotel.com/
We Boutique Hotel Map
https://goo.gl/maps/vhdt78rAXWt

## Casa Bella Gracia

This nice budget hotel is away from all the crowds of Barcelona and will give you a cosy hideout when visiting Barcelona.The location is in the village of Gracia and will give you a sense of being in traditional Barcelona with its small streets and fantastic atmosphere.Casa Bella Gracia is a modern hotel with a nice warm feeling to it.The hotel only has 12 rooms and has a lovely roof terrace for having a cup of coffee or breakfast.

Address:Carrer de Sant Agustí, 4, Barcelona
Phone:+34 638 49 34 28
Casa Bella Gracia Website
http://www.casabellagracia.com/en
Casa Bella Gracia Map
https://goo.gl/maps/g5Zh9zCb8J72

## Praktik Bakery, Eixample Dreta

Praktik Bakery Hotel is a unique hotel concept in Barcelona where a hotel and bakery has teamed up.You have the rooms on the upper floors and the bakery on the ground floor.The rooms are not very big but it has everything you need and the great thing is you can just go downstairs and grab a coffee and fantastic fresh bread.

Address:Carrer de Provença, 279,Barcelona
Phone:+34 934 88 00 61
Praktik Bakery Hotel Website

http://www.hotelpraktikbakery.com/
Praktik Bakery Hotel Map
https://goo.gl/maps/9SdRwwxWLM92

## Hotel Ciutat De Barcelona

Hotel Ciutat De Barcelona is located in the beautiful Born neighbourhood.This hotel is very basic but has great service and a very nice rooftop terrace with a pool.For a budget hotel, this is a very good deal and is located in one of the best neighborhoods in Barcelona.

Address: Carrer de la Princesa, 33 – 35, Barcelona
Phone:+34 932 69 74 75
Hotel Ciutat De Barcelona
http://www.ciutatbarcelona.com/
Hotel Ciutat De Barcelona
https://goo.gl/maps/D8gea8UU4FU2

## Hotel Pulitzer

If you want to stay in a central location in Barcelona, and you don't mind the crowds, then this is good hotel for your stay.Although this area has a reputation for being a party area the hotel is fantastic and will give you a nice peaceful base away from the busy Barcelona streets.The hotel has a great design, and it has a very nice lobby with white leather sofas to take a break from your busy day in Barcelona.

Address: Carrer de Bergara, 8,Barcelona
Phone:+34 934 81 67 67
Hotel Pulitzer
http://www.hotelpulitzer.es/en/we/
Hotel Pulitzer
https://goo.gl/maps/v4H6KgGtY2u

# 17

# Getting to know Barcelona

## Las Ramblas

There is no doubt that when you visit Barcelona, one of the first things that will come to your mind is that it is a modern city. It's not completely modern, but it mixes some of the traditional with the new. You get to see that up close and personal in Las Ramblas.

There is usually a lot of traffic in this part of the city. Well, not exactly vehicular traffic. You only get foot traffic in this part of the woods. You can say that this is the most popular street (yes, it's a street) in Barcelona.

People sometimes call it La Rambla, note that that is a singular term. Well, that is also politically correct since it does look like just one long stretch of a boulevard. However, calling it Las Ramblas (the plural one) is also correct.

You see, it's not really just one street; it's five streets in a row. The name actually describes a stretch of five boulevards all lined up into a pretty long promenade. If you look hard enough (and if you have a map of the city), you can discover for yourself that the long boulevard starts with Placa Catalunya and it ends somewhere near the waterfront where the Columbus Statue is located.

Literally hundreds of people take a leisurely stroll on this two kilometer stretch of road. They enjoy the many historic landmarks along the way. They also get to try the many delicacies the city has to offer through the many shops lined up along the way.

You can do some souvenir shopping, enjoy some of the local color and watch street performers do their thing. Visitors can sit back and relax and enjoy some of that famous coffee that others have been raving about. It's a place where you can mingle with the people in what is arguably the most popular boulevard in all of Spain.

To get to Las Ramblas take the subway to Plaça de Catalunya Metro Station.

Las Ramblas Map
https://goo.gl/maps/UMYTJ9Py4Xt

## Parc de la Ciutadella

Yes, this is a park, and it's also a historic place. Back in the day, this was once a fort; the name Ciutadella can be translated into "citadel." This is one of the most popular landmarks in the whole of lower Barcelona.

If you're a nature lover, then you will enjoy the pair of botanical gardens situated right here. Here, you will also find what people call La Cascada. These are two fountains designed by no other than the renowned architect Gaudi.

There is a lake where you can go rowing and enjoy the serene atmosphere. The huge statue of an elephant is also a nice place to take a selfie. Another attraction in Ciutadella is the Castell dels Tres Dragons (literally Castle of Three Dragons) and a zoo. If you're visiting Barcelona and you have kids with you, then this is a good place you should not miss especially if you only have a couple of days to spare.

To get here take the subway to Ciutadella-Vila Olímpica Metro Station

Parc de la Ciutadella Map
https://goo.gl/maps/q1dCmzcbmRT2

### Sagrada Familia

If you like visiting ancient churches and if you like to see architecture that you probably haven't seen before, then make it a point to stop by Sagrada Familia. Not only is this unique architectural marvel a thing that can make your breath stop, its design is also attributed to the now immortalized Antoni Gaudi.

A little tidbit of info here is the fact that Gaudi was not the original craftsman who was commissioned by royalty to oversee the construction of Sagrada Familia. It was originally given to Francisco

de Paula del Villar, another famous architect.

Unfortunately, Villar wasn't able to complete the project since he was getting old. He retired in March 18, 1883 and the remainder of the work was given to Gaudi. The man then made a lot of drastic changes. These radical improvements were authentic and original. It's also one of the big reasons why the place is quite popular with tourists.

To get here take the subway to Sagrada Família Metro Station

Address: Carrer de Mallorca, 401, Barcelona
Phone:+34 932 08 04 14
Sagrada Família Website
http://www.sagradafamilia.org/
Sagrada Familia Map
https://goo.gl/maps/y47pfYMkMxu

## La Ribera

Do you want to know how it feels like to live during medieval times? If that is the kind of thing you're into, then you're in luck. La Ribera offers just that. It is located on the western section of what is known as Ciutat Vella.

The name La Ribera can be literally translated into "the shore," which is basically where the place is situated. Go to the southernmost side of the place, and you'll find the sea right there.

Here, you will find a lot of traditional shops, which includes some weaver's shops (Carrer Cotoners), as well as rope making shops (Carrer Corders). Weavings and ropes aren't big industries nowadays, but they were important businesses in ancient times. Other than that, some of the more traditional shops you'll find here include mirror forgers and glazers.

Other than the entire section of medieval merchants (a great place to get some souvenirs you can brag about when you get home), you'll also find a lot of museums along the way. It's a great place to teach your kids some ancient European history. It's also a good way to appreciate life then and be thankful for the comforts of modern living.

To get here take the subway to Jaume I Metro Station

Address: Plaça Comercial, 11, Barcelona

Phone:+34 933 19 52 06
La Ribera Website
http://www.laribera.cat/
La Ribera Map
https://goo.gl/maps/kyKn3LCAsyk

## La Placa de Catalunya

One way or another you will have to get to La Plaça de Catalunya. Well, this is the main transport hub of all of Barcelona. If you need to travel anywhere and you want to get a ride, then this is where you go to get one. Different forms of public transport can be found here – unless of course you prefer to travel on foot.

Since all the streets in Barcelona follow a rigid grid-like pattern, you will notice that all of the major routes will eventually lead here. It's like the hub of a wheel and all roads pass by this center. It's interesting that some people just call it "the square" (well if you look at a map, it will resemble some sort of a square right in the middle of the city).

This road and city design is the work of Ildefons Cerdà i Sunyer(Urban Planner) who was devising some sort of a utopian city plan. The way roads are designed, making extensions and expansions won't be a huge problem. The design also permits enough sunlight and ventilation to every city quarter. Now that is architecture with brilliant insight.

To get here take the subway to Plaça de Catalunya Metro Station

Address: Plaça de Catalunya,Barcelona
La Placa de Catalunya Map
https://goo.gl/maps/GzzpuKXpdyt

### Tèxtil Café

Okay, so all that walking and all the medieval stuff can clog your memory so you ought to take a break, and one of the best places to do just that is Tèxtil Café. Here, you'll be enticed to order what the other people are having.

The seating is rather elegant no matter what time of the year it is. You can enjoy a light snack consisting of local pastries and a local brewed cup of coffee. The best part is that you're stretching your legs under the patio of a 14th-century mansion.

It's perfectly situated near two other famous landmarks, namely Museu Picasso (Picasso Museum) and Museu Tèxtil. Expect to meet other tourists and many locals here. You can enjoy the eclectic atmosphere and be on your way to continue on with your journey after a rather refreshing cup.

To get here take the subway to Jaume I Metro Station

Address: Carrer de Montcada, 12, Barcelona
Tèxtil Café Map
https://goo.gl/maps/dhvbitTbxe32

### Marina Port Vell

Would you be interested in riding a yacht? You can actually book a day trip where you sail a classic yacht and travel along the city's coastline. It's a really adventurous and somewhat romantic thing to do. It's not anything like an extreme sport, but it's more of a relaxed and rather toned down way to enjoy the sea and the beautiful coast.

You won't believe it if one of the locals would tell you that Marina Port Vell didn't look as sublime a few years back. It was nothing but drab prior to 1992. Most of the place contained nothing more than piles upon piles of containers.

This was once part of the industrial zone. Nowadays, it has been transformed into a beautiful beach side with promenades along its path. This is also a great place to see some of the city's nightlife.

Here, you'll find the Moll d'Espanya with its famous but exclusive Club Marítim. You will have to make arrangements if you want to enter. However, making the extra effort will be worth your while.

There is also an IMAX cinema here where visitors can enjoy a movie together. If you're bringing kids along for the boat ride, they may want to visit the aquarium after you've had your lunch. There are also a lot of places of interest nearby.

Some of the other tourist attractions here include Reials Drassanes, which is the 14th century Royal Shipyards, the city's World Trade Center, the Moll de Barcelona, and the Torre de Jaume I.

To get here take the subway to Liceu Metro station.
Address: l'Escar, 26 (The Gallery Building), Carrer de l'Escar, Barcelona
Phone:+34 934 84 23 00
Marina Port VellWebsite
http://www.oneoceanportvell.com/
Marina Port Vell Map
https://goo.gl/maps/8zt6RYRWTWP2

## La Barceloneta and Port Olímpic
Have you ever wondered what the local street food tastes like? If you're a bit of an adventurer when it comes to tastes and flavors, then you might want to try the chiringuitos they sell here. Don't worry, they're safe to eat and won't upset your stomach.

They're basically just snacks and a lot of it should be seafood. This part of the city used to be an 18th century area where the working class lived. It used to be a downtrodden area but has since been transformed into a place where both locals and tourists can have a nice walk.

Another interesting thing that the locals do here is that this is where they walk their dogs. If you're looking for some of the best places to eat, then make it a point to visit this part of the city. You'll also spot some of the best nightlife the city has to offer.

To get here take the subway to Barceloneta Metro Station.

La Barceloneta Map
https://goo.gl/maps/hTpYkFrZJbA2

Address: Edificio de Capitanía, S/N,Barcelona
Phone:+34 932 25 92 20
Port Olímpic Website
http://www.portolimpic.es/presentacion.php?i=3
Port Olímpic Map
https://goo.gl/maps/uH5VdaHJTpL2

### Santa María del Mar

Can't have enough of the old world architecture? Then see one of the city's finest in Santa María del Mar. It comes complete with stained glass windows, high steep vaults and the embrace of the nearby Mediterranean shore. That's a really picturesque view considering everything.

Some have said that this is one of the most well-preserved monuments that depict gothic architecture. The best part of it all is that you won't see the usual crowd gathering here. It's a great place to feel solemnity and be alone with your soul.

To get here take the subway to Jaume I Metro Station.

Address: Plaça de Santa Maria, 1, Barcelona
Phone:+34 933 10 23 90
Santa María del Mar Website
http://www.santamariadelmarbarcelona.org/home/
Santa María del Mar Map
https://goo.gl/maps/dG7oxqaLFXF2

# 18

# Museums

Visiting a museum will transport you to various exciting times in history. It allows you to get to know your roots. It also allows you to enrich your knowledge about history.

Barcelona is a haven of many beautiful and rich museums. It is filled with fantastic and inspiring museums that will mesmerize you.

When you are in Barcelona, it is a must to visit the following museums:

### Museu d' Historia de la Ciutat

This is THE city museum of Barcelona and it is for the ancient history buffs. You the entrance to this magnificent museum is through a beautiful 16th century mansion called Casa Padellas. Then you can walk past to the ancient Roman city of Barcino which is located in the underground levels of the museum. Here, you will discover the remains of the Placa Del Rei, a medieval royal palace.

Here are some of the places that you should visit when touring inside this museum:
- Roman funeral way
- Temple of Augustus
- Roman Domus of Saint Honorat

- Villa Joana
- Turo de la Rovira
- Outstaning Catalan Persons Gallery

Address:Plaça del Rei, s/n, Barcelona
Phone:+34 932 56 21 00
Museu d' Historia de la Ciutat Website
http://museuhistoria.bcn.cat/
Museu d' Historia de la Ciutat Map
https://goo.gl/maps/sQ5QqEPs3sB2

### Museu Barbier-Mueller d'Art Pre-Colombi

This is a museum that is dedicated to pre-columbian art and cultures of South and Central America. You could find many precious South American jewelries in this museum. You will also find various statues, textiles, and ceramics.

Address:Carrer de Montcada, 14,Barcelona
Phone:+34 933 10 45 16
Museu Barbier-Mueller d'Art Pre-Colombi Website
http://www.barbier-mueller.ch/?lang=es
Museu Barbier-Mueller d'Art Pre-Colombi Map
https://goo.gl/maps/LBbHRmRFpn82

### Museu de la Xocolata

If you love chocolate, then you should visit this museum. The Museu de la Xocolata is for kids and kids at heart. It is also for hard core chocoholics. This museum will allow you to trace the history of chocolate.

You can also find chocolate models of anythings from grand tourists attractions such as the La Sagrada Familia to beloved cartoon characters such as Sponge Bob, Tom and Jerry, and Winnie the Pooh. Kids will surely have fun inside "The Chocolate Museum".

Address:Carrer del Comerç, 36,Barcelona
Phone:+34 932 68 78 78
Museu de la Xocolata Website
http://www.museuxocolata.cat/?lang=en
Museu de la Xocolata Map
https://goo.gl/maps/7B7PfVJmSry

### Museo del Perfume (Museum of Perfume)
Barcelona is a city full of special things to do.The Museum of perfume is one of the places that you have to visit.The museum has a wide variety of perfumes that date back to ancient times.This shop is a bit tricky to find because it's located at the back of a big perfume shop, but its worth a visit.

Address: Passeig de Gràcia, 39,Barcelona
Phone:+34 932 16 01 21
Museo del Perfume Website
http://www.museudelperfum.com/
Museo del Perfume Map
https://goo.gl/maps/3rUm5qfYqn92

### Picasso Museum
There are not many people in the world that do not know who Picasso was.He is one of the greatest artists in History.This museum has one of the biggest collections of Picasso's work in the world.

There's no arguing about it, this is the most popular art museum in all of Barcelona. You put the name of Pablo Picasso on it and you should expect people to crowd around to appreciate the man's genius.

The Picasso Museum is located at the very heart of what is known as La Ribera.

It's surrounded by five old mansions that create an elegant old world atmosphere, which is quite rare nowadays. Even if you're not an art enthusiast, you will appreciate the collections they have on display here. The ones you'll find here are Picasso's more conventional works.

Picasso first set foot on this land way back in 1895. He arrived with his family. He immediately put up a studio, which was a pretty bold move at the time. The studio, if you're interested, can be found in Carrer de la Plata.

Here are some of the notable buildings that are occupied by the museum:
- Palau Aguilar – This is the first building that is occupied by the museum.
- Palau Meca – This palace has a beautiful central courtyard. It also has a polychrome coffered ceiling.
- Palau Finestres – This building was built in 1363 and it is currently used as an exhibition place.
- Casa Mauri – This building was acquired by Museu Picasso in 1999.

Address: Carrer Montcada, 15-23,Barcelona
Phone:+34 932 56 30 00
Picasso Museum Website
http://www.museupicasso.bcn.cat/
Picasso Museum Map
https://goo.gl/maps/fDUw9PqfTZx

## National Art Museum of Catalonia Barcelona

This gallery focuses on Catalan visual art.The museum has a wide variety of artwork.There are different sections that focus on the Romanesque art, Gothic art, Renaissance art, Baroque art and Modern art.

Address: Palau Nacional, Parc de Montjuïc, s/n,Barcelona, Phone:+34 936 22 03 60
National Art Museum of Catalonia Barcelona Website
http://museunacional.cat/en/getting-here
National Art Museum of Catalonia Barcelona Map
https://goo.gl/maps/VcoMKqSKzMm

## Barcelona Museum of Contemporary Art

Your trip to Barcelona has to include a visit to this museum.The big collections that can be seen here is very special.The museum focuses on three periods,the 1940's - 1960's,1960's - 1970's,the last period is contemporary.

Address: Plaça dels Àngels, 1, 08001 Barcelona
Phone:+34 934 12 08 10
Barcelona Museum of Contemporary Art Website
http://www.macba.cat/
Barcelona Museum of Contemporary Art Map
https://goo.gl/maps/nhghn4zxpk82

## Museu Marítim

If you appreciate gothic art and architecture, then you will love what you will find in the Museu Marítim. It's near the Royal Shipyards, and it is a Naval Museum. You'll find here collections that testify of the glory of the old naval history of Barcelona.

One particular collection to note is the Great Adventure of the Sea. It's one of the more popular attractions here. It also includes miniatures of the ships that Ferdinand Magellan used to circumnavigate the world. As an ending note to the tour, you can get onboard one of the ships, the Santa Eulàlia, an ancient sailing ship that is currently sitting on the Moll de la Fusta.

Address:Av. de les Drassanes, s/n,Barcelona
Phone:+34 933 42 99 20
Museu Marítim Website
http://www.mmb.cat/
Museu Marítim Map
https://goo.gl/maps/DtUZUiqy2E92

# 19

# Art Galleries in Barcelona

Aside from the museums, Barcelona also houses the most exquisite art galleries.

Here are some of the most interesting and art galleries in Barcelona:

### Galeria Joan Prats
This is one of the pioneering art galleries in Barcelona. It was built and founded in 1976 and it is part of several popular art fairs like Arco and Art Basel in Miami Beach. It showcases contemporary art and it houses the work of various artists like Erck Beltran, Knut Asdam, Carla Zaccagnini, Carles Congost, and Hannah Collins.

Address:Balmes 54, 08007 Barcelona,
Phone:+34 932 16 02 90
Galeria Joan Prats Website
http://www.galeriajoanprats.com/
Galeria Joan Prats Map
https://goo.gl/maps/dGmqCg64mWz

### Marlborough
Marlborough is one of the most popular art dealers in the word. It was initially founded in London and it showcases the art work of artists like Francis Bacon, Henry Moore, Oskar Kokoschka, and Victor

Pasmore.

Address:Carrer d'Enric Granados, 68,Barcelona
Phone:+34 934 67 44 54
Marlborough Website
http://www.galeriamarlborough.com/
Marlborough Map
https://goo.gl/maps/o7UJYhnxVvQ2

## AB Galeria D'Art

The AB (Antoni Botey) Gallery of Art houses the fantastic work of both established and up-and-coming artists. This gallery showcases the work of Carles Vives, Vicenc Viaplana, Josep Ucles, Josep Maria Subirachs, Joan Ponc, Pablo Picasso, Marc Petit, Manolo Moreno, Ara Mikaelan, Josep Guinovart, Jaume Guinovart, Pere Galera, Margarita Escalas, Modest Cuixart, Jordi Cerda, Joaquim Camp, Josep Bofill, Erwing Bechtold, Eduard Arranz Bravo, and other established artists.

Address:Carrer Agustí Vinyamata, 55,Granollers, Barcelona
Phone:+34 938 70 73 52
AB Galeria D'Art Website
http://www.abgaleriadart.com/galeria/
AB Galeria D'Art Map
https://goo.gl/maps/99uvXY85cN72

## Ambit Galeria D'Art

This gallery showcases contemporary art of established artists from Spain and from other parts of the world. This gallery showcases the art work of notable artists like Artur Heras, Fernando Cartes, Eaves Casamada, Xavier Franquesa, Perico Pastor, Josep Codina, Ignacio Bugos, JP Viladecans, Franco Monti, Carmen Garolera, Riccardo Licata, and Ramon Enrich.

Address:Carrer del Consell de Cent, 282, Barcelona
Phone:+34 934 88 18 00
Ambit Galeria D'Art Website
http://ambitgaleriaart.com/
Ambit Galeria D'Art Map
https://goo.gl/maps/AKiybRPFaCx

**Artevistas Gallery**
This hip gallery showcases the contemporary work of various artists like the following:

- Albert Blanchart
- Andrea Torres Balaguer
- Cane
- Chimera
- C. Llonch
- Asis Percales
- F. Diamond
- Laura Armato
- Gil Gelpi
- Irene Bou
- Gori Mora
- Lantonio
- Otero
- Peta
- Monika Gojer
- Marcel Rodriguez
- R. Elizegi
- Nuria Torres
- Nicolas Rico
- Kyle Bryant
- Zachari Logan
- Sergi Perez

- Pablo del Pozo
- Jey Alonzo

Address:Passatge del Crèdit, 4,Barcelona
Phone:+34 935 13 04 65
Artevistas Gallery Website
http://www.artevistas-gallery.com/en_GB
Artevistas Gallery Map
https://goo.gl/maps/TrAphvqujQr

### Galeria A. Cortina

This gallery contains unique and beautiful modern and contemporary art. This art gallery was founded in 1981. This gallery showcases and deals the works of Miguel Barcelo, Francisco Bores, Maria Blanchard, Manolo Millares, Carlos Nadal, Albert Rafols Casamada, Pablo Picasso, Eduardo Chillida, Salvador Dali, Modest Cuixart, and many more.

Address:Carrer de València, 248,Barcelona
Phone:+34 934 87 68 86
Galeria A. Cortina Website
http://www.galeriacortina.com/
Galeria A. Cortina Map
https://goo.gl/maps/DEE5pGMGogA2

### Agora 3 Galeria d'Art

This gallery features contemporary figurative artists of the 20th century. It showcases the work of Yolanda Martin, H. Tran, Joan Iriarte, Grau Santos, A. Alemany, T. Llacer, M.A. Soler, J. Balaguer,

Nory Steiger, and J. Veciana.

This gallery is open from Tuesday to Saturday 11 am to 2 pm and 4 pm to 8 pm. It is also open on Sundays from 11 am to 2 pm.

Address:Carrer Nou, 20, 08870 Sitges, Barcelona

Phone:+34 938 94 03 38

Agora 3 Galeria d'Art Website

http://www.agora.es/

Agora 3 Galeria d'Art Map

https://goo.gl/maps/VRZibNLw1nS2

# 20

# Where to Eat in Barcelona?

In Spain, all the items on the menu will be listed. Remember that you can't change anything on the menu, and you rarely can create your own courses (or add another course to your meals).

One important thing you should take note of is that most of the restaurants will be closed on 4 pm and will resume business at 8 pm. Shop and restaurant owners usually take siesta in the afternoon. In case you don't want to go hungry during the said times, better buy a snack you can carry with you.

However, there are international chains as well as other local restaurants that do accommodate tourists during siesta. If you find one along the way, then make a mental note (or better yet, write it down on your itinerary) of the place. In case you get hungry while visiting the different places in the city, then you can come back to the restaurant and have a full meal.

## What Dishes do they Serve?

Don't fret if a lot of the dishes you'll be offered is no other than seafood. You're in the Mediterranean and so expect Mediterranean meals. Well, it does have a good mix of veggies and fruits so you are actually getting a healthy meal for your money.

You should, however, take note that the seafood here isn't particularly local. That's another setback when you convert an entire city to tourism. Among the items unique to the local cuisine are tapas that are usually sold in bars as well.

It's not a particularly healthy meaty helping, but it is definitely flavorful. Unfortunately, it's not cheap, so be prepared to pay extra for something that tastes great. Another thing you will also notice here is that many street stands sell waffles.

Most tourist guides won't tell you this, and you'll be left to discover this fact on your own. If you love waffles, you should try the ones sold here. They are a good striking contrast to the Belgian waffles that most people are used to eating. They smell great and they do taste just as good too.

## So How Much Do I Pay for a Meal?

Food prices in any part of the world will tend to fluctuate. It doesn't matter whether you're in Barcelona or not. However, just to give you a rough estimate, a budget meal for one person in this city will cost something like 10 Euros. A mid-range meal for a single individual (which includes a drink) will cost up to 25 Euros. If you spend more money on food (above 25 Euros), then that is considered splurging.

## Where to Find the Good Restaurants?

The really great restaurants can be found all over Barcelona. However, there are some places where you can find many clusters of food places, bars and restaurants where they serve scrumptious meals.

## Barceloneta

One popular area even for the locals is known as Barceloneta. If you've become a fan of the local baked fish dish, then this is where you'll find some of its best versions. The dish is locally known as Paella. Another popular local dish is Arròs negre, which is a helping of black rice.

Barceloneta Map
https://goo.gl/maps/1tDgqLPhd4w

There are other sections of the city where you can find the good places to eat. That includes Eixample Esquerra, which is located between Gran Via and the famous Mallorca. Plaça Catalunya also has a good selection of restaurants you might want to try. Another good place to check out is El Born, which you will find right next to Barri Gòtic, another good place to sample the local cuisine.

· Eixample Esquerra
· Plaça Catalunya
· El Born
· Barri Gòtic

## Restaurants
### Can Costa

Since we have already mentioned Barceloneta, one particular place you might want to have your meal is Can Costa. If you love seafood, then this is where you might find your heart's delight. The place is located along Passeig de Joan de Borbón, which is pretty hard to miss.

If you find yourself lost, just look for the waterfront and then walk back one block and you'll see Can Costa right away. It's not really that hard to find. There is one important detail you should take note of; this is the place where the locals usually eat. This says everything you need to know about this restaurant.

If you relish in sampling the local cuisine, then try one of their highly recommended dishes, fideuà de paella. Yes, it's another baked fish dish but don't get disappointed. If you're dying for the genuine Catalan baked fish dish, then this is it. Notice, this dish doesn't incorporate rice – instead it has noodles!

If you can't have enough of the seafood served here, then make sure you order one of their baby calamaris. That's squid fried with breading. Remeber is that you should arrive here some time before 2 pm, or else you won't find a table. The place is quite popular, and there's no guarantee that you can reserve some seats.

Address:Passeig de Joan de Borbó, 70
Phone:+34 932 21 59 03
Website
http://www.restaurantecancosta.com/
Can Costa Map
https://goo.gl/maps/VVA9iw5JMLx

### Bar Marsella

Another popular place to eat is Bar Marsella. It is located on Carrer Sant Pau 65. If you're looking for true blue Catalan meals, then this is another great place to get just that. You'll also appreciate the décor. Much of it is 19th century, which includes rafters, really classic heavy drapes and chandeliers hanging way up in the ceiling.

To get here take the subway to Liceu Metro.
Address:Carrer de Sant Pau, 65
Phone:+34 934 42 72 63
Bar Marsella Map
https://goo.gl/maps/PgX43trLdvw

## Set Portes

This is a classic old paella and seafood restaurant.This place has an amazing atmosphere and has been in Barcelona since 1836.The food here is amazing.

To get here take the subway to Metro Barceloneta.
Address:Passeig Isabel II, 14,
Phone:+34 933 19 30 33
Website
http://7portes.com/
Set Portes Map
https://goo.gl/maps/YhsoYyDvoCM2

## Can Culleretes

Can Culleretes is one of the oldest restaurants in Spain and has ben around since 1786.Amazing food and great atmosphere.They serve a variety of traditional spanish dishes.

To get there take the subway to Metro Liceu.
Address:Carrer d'en Quintana, 5
Phone:+34 933 17 30 22

Website
http://www.culleretes.com/
Can Culleretes Map
https://goo.gl/maps/qQctvTnmpL12

# 21

# Coffee Shops

Barcelona has many coffee shops and bars. If you are looking to have a relaxing time, it is best to stroll around the streets of Barcelona and discover the hip and classy coffee shops and bars in this magnificent city.

Here are some of the best coffee and pastry shops that you should visit while you are in Barcelona:

## Café Salambo

This café is famous local landmark in Gracia. This is a perfect place to have cocktails and coffee with your friends. This café has a wide selection of cocktails like the Mexic (tequila, cream, and chilli), Roma (grappa and cream), and the Bombo (chocolate, condensed milk, and Cointreau).

Address:Carrer de Torrijos, 51
Phone:+34 932 18 69 66
Website
http://www.cafesalambo.com/
Café Salambo Map
https://goo.gl/maps/ALyrbN75rUG2

## Cafes el Magnifico

This coffee shop has a tasting area where you can sample some of their delicious and well-prepared coffee drinks. You can also buy the best coffee beans in the world in this café. This coffee shop serves the best cappuccinos.

Address:Carrer de l'Argenteria, 64
Phone:+34 933 19 39 75
Website
http://www.cafeselmagnifico.com/
Cafes el Magnifico Map
https://goo.gl/maps/NGhjhLMMpHt

## Cachitos

This cozy café has an elaborate and striking décor. But, it offers a great experience. Aside from coffee, this café serves a variety of dishes that are made of premium ingredients. This café also have good wines and cocktails.

Address:Rambla de Catalunya, 33
Phone:+34 932 15 27 18
Website
http://www.cachitosrambla.com/#inicio
Cachitos Map
https://goo.gl/maps/W57MjMFkhkC2

## Caelum

This café has the best parties in Barcelona. They sell different kind of sweet treats that are made by nuns and monks in convents and monasteries all around Catalonia. This café also have a good selection of teas.

Address:Carrer de la Palla, 8
Phone:+34 933 02 69 93
Website
http://www.caelumbarcelona.com/
Caelum Map
https://goo.gl/maps/bgfMDENxvuz

## Meson del Café

This place serves great coffee but you will be mesmerized by its ambience. This café and bar was founded in 1909. They serve great pastries and they serve delicious hot chocolate, too. This café will surely give you a different kind of experience.
Address:Carrer de la Llibreteria, 16
Phone:+34 933 15 07 54
Meson del Café Map
https://goo.gl/maps/js5kdUCmQKp

# 22

# Bars

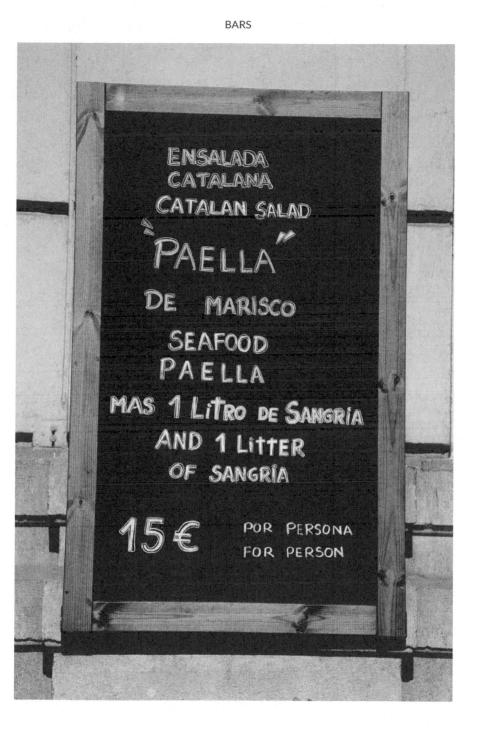

Here are the best bars that you should visit while you are in Barcelona:

## Chill

Many young professionals love to visit this bar for coffee and drinks.Live DJ's and theme parties are hosted here.During the day Cafe Chill is a great place to meet for a cup of coffee.

Address:Carrer de Provença, 424
Phone:+34 934 76 22 70
Website
http://www.chillbarcelona.com/
Chill Map
https://goo.gl/maps/m8kf9opMXa52

## L'Entresol
This bar is perfect for gin tonic lovers. This bar feels like a paradise. The decoration of this café is impressive. The place is painted with a great combination of red, white, and black colors. You can also find old picture frames on the wall. It also has great music selection. This bar plays funky, groove, and indie music.

Address:Carrer del Planeta, 39
Phone:+34 685 53 39 41
L'Entresol Map
https://goo.gl/maps/oA3uE653QVM2

## Never Mind
This is a fun rock and roll bar with a 90's grunge theme.This place is a favorite with university students.The bar is great for a fun late night out with friends or alone.

Address:Escudellers Blancs N°3 Bajos
Phone:+34 678 55 01 52
Website

https://www.facebook.com/NevermindBcn
Never Mind Map
https://goo.gl/maps/6pYGPYP9pQH2

## Xixbar

Barcelona locals love this bar so you have to visit it as well. This bar is an old dairy house that now serves the best tonics and gins in Barcelona. The tonics and gin served in this bar mixed with different ginger, cinnamon, mint, cucumber, and berries. This bar organizes several fun tasting events.

Address:Carrer de Rocafort, 19
Phone:+34 934 23 43 14
Website
http://www.xixbar.com/
Xixbar Map
https://goo.gl/maps/YLaRgsqA5jQ2

# 23

# Barcelona's Festivals

Another reason why people visit Barcelona is their illustrious festivities. You can time your trip to the city and arrive just when one of these lively fiestas are on schedule. That way you get to witness everything first hand. Note that these fiestas are unique to Catalonia, which means you'll never even see them celebrated elsewhere in Spain.

## Cavalcada de Reis

This is one of the very first festivities on schedule each year. It is celebrated on January 5th of each year. It's one of the festivities especially geared for children so you might want to bring your kids along for the trip. The highlight of this fiesta is the travel of the three wise men with lots of heavily decorated floats and street dancing.

## Sónar

Are you a music lover? Then this is one of the festivities you shouldn't miss. The festivity doesn't only feature the local music. It also highlights advanced multimedia arts. It's not just for ancient and folk music, you'll enjoy the best music in the city as well.

## Sant Jordi

Do you want to propose to the girl of your dreams? Do you want to make it during one of the most romantic events in the world? Then bring your girl to Barcelona during Sant Jordi. Don't forget the ring!

Walk around Barcelona during Sant Jordi and don't be surprised if the locals shower you with flowers. This is their equivalent of Valentine's Day. Take note that it is customary for men to give flowers to women and women give books to the men. Sant Jordi is celebrated on April 23 of each year.

## Fira de Santa Llúcia

If you want to celebrate a different Christmas with your loved ones, then try spending the holiday season here in Barcelona. You'll get to witness Fira de Santa Llúcia. This festival is scheduled on December 13th of each year and the entire week leading to Christmas is usually festive. It's like having an entire week with the Christmas spirit in your heart.

### Revetlla de Sant Joan

If you enjoy fireworks, then you will love Revetlla de Sant Joan. This fiesta celebrates the midsummer solstice and is quite festive. It is celebrated on June 23rd of each year, and fireworks usually light up the night sky 24/7. It's a night of festivities and a time to party the night away.

### La Mercè

This feast is rather solemn and is celebrated on September 24th of every year. This is actually one of the oldest feasts in Barcelona. It dates all the way back to the 17th century. It features a lot of parades, music events, fireworks and magic fountain activities. The best part is that on the last night everyone gets to have all they want of Barcelona's local liquor known as Cava.

Now, these are only some of the many festivals that are held year round. Remember to schedule your trip carefully. Take note of the different places of interest and have a rowdy good time when you visit Barcelona.

# 24

# Things that You Can Only Do in Barcelona

Traveling to Barcelona will give you great and exciting memories. Barcelona is a city like no other, and there are things that you can only do in Barcelona.

Here are some of the activities that you can do while you are in Barcelona:

**(1) Have dinner and stroll on Las Ramblas**

Las Ramblas is the main tourist destination in Barcelona. This 1.2-kilometer pedestrian stress is packed with souvenir shops, cafes, restaurants, hawkers, and street performers. Here are some of the major attractions in Las Ramblas:

### Erotica Museum
Address:La Rambla, 96 bis
Phone:+34 933 18 98 65
Erotica Museum Map
https://goo.gl/maps/6QsEscL1dUH2

### Barcelona Wax Museum
Address:Passatge de la Banca, 7
Phone:+34 933 17 26 49
Barcelona Wax Museum Map
https://goo.gl/maps/BhDSMBooKs92

### Modernist Boqueria Market
Address:La Rambla, 91
Phone:+34 933 18 25 84
Modernist Boqueria Market Map
https://goo.gl/maps/A6FM8vNQh5C2

### Christopher Columbus Monument
Address:Plaça Portal de la pau, s/n
Phone:+34 932 85 38 32
Christopher Columbus Monument Map
https://goo.gl/maps/hw7JBoomQkJ2

### White Painter Statue
Address:Passeig de Colom, s/n

White Painter Statue Map
https://goo.gl/maps/zKimT1gnn7s

You can also find the mosaic by Joan Miro within the promenade in Las Ramblas. You can find various flower shops where you can find unique and fresh flowers.

It is also a must to set aside a few hours to go around La Boquera. This is one of the oldest market in Barcelona and in Spain. You can find a wide variety of fruits. It is also a must to buy the traditional sausages and chorizo. Also, don't forget to enjoy and beautiful stained glass and Art Nouveau architecture in the market.

### (2) Ride the "Steel Donkey".
Of course, the term "steel donkey" is a euphemism for a bicycle. You can go on a bike tour in Barcelona. But, the Steel Donkey Bike tour is not your ordinary bike tour.

When you go on a Steel Donkey Bike Tour, you'll visit the charming back streets the village district of Gracia, the old industrial ruins of Poblenou, and the back streets of El Bourne. You can find many many flea markets, squat houses, and recycled workshops while you are on this bike tour.

Address:The Green Bike Shop, Carrer Ample 53
Phone:+34 657286854
Email: info@steeldonkeybiketours.com
Website
http://www.steeldonkeybiketours.com/
Steel Donkey Map
https://goo.gl/maps/hpYxQ3zPUsy

### (3) Get Electric on A Bicycle
Aside from the standard Steel Donkey Bike tour, you can also go on an e-bike tour. It is a memorable experience where you get to have fun racing with city cars, too.

Address:Carrer de Montsió, 10
Phone:+34 902 02 77 20
Bicycle Website
http://www.barcelonaebikes.com/en/
E-bike Map
https://goo.gl/maps/v7j2MDBEoaJ2

### (4) See Madonna on a Magic Hill
You can visit the image of Virgin Mary called Black Madonna in Barcelona. This statue is located at the Montserrat Abbey in the high peaks of Montserrat Mountain. Many pilgrims from all over the world go up in the high mountains to see this statue. But, many people travel to Montserrat Mountain for other reasons. This "jagged" mountain has a breathtaking view. You can also go on wine tour near the Montserrat mountain.

Phone:+34 938 77 77 77
Website
https://www.montserrat-tourist-guide.com/
Black Madonna Map
https://goo.gl/maps/Zvkj893xpt12

## (5) Go on a Barcelona Booze Cruise

You can go on a Barcelona Booze Cruise and drink like a sailor! When you go on a Barcelona Booze Cruise, you will enjoy tasty barbeque, beer, sangria, and cocktails. You can also enjoy the music of resident DJs and games. The Barcelona Booze Cruise is definitely for party animals.

Phone:(+34)602 660 736
info@boozecruisebarcelona.com
Booze Cruise Website
http://www.boozecruisebarcelona.com/

## (6) Drive a Ferrari Around an F1 Circuit

It is not every day that you get to drive a Ferrari and it is definitely not every day that you get to drive around the Circuit de Catalunya which is the official track of the Spanish F1 Grand Prix. Well, the good news is, you can do this in Barcelona. You can also pretend that you are James Bond while you are driving on the way to Monte Carl.

Address:Camino Mas Moreneta
Phone:938864451
Website
http://en.circuitcatexperience.com/
F1 Circuit Map
https://goo.gl/maps/57Pp9NudpG52

## (7) Dine in a Dark Area

The famous Dance Le Noir? is not your ordinary restaurant. This restaurant will provide a great sensory experience because in here, you will eat your dinner in a lightless room. Most of the restaurant's waiters are blind. The food is great and if you want to try something different with your friends, you should have dinner in Dance Le Noir?. Dining in this restaurant is definitely a memorable experience.

Address:Passeig de Picasso, 10
Phone:+34 932 68 70 17
Website
http://barcelona.danslenoir.com/
Dance Le Noir Map
https://goo.gl/maps/7UbJnrxDte22

### (8)Cover your body with chocolate!

Barcelona is a city of pleasure. It is a must to get a massage in Barcelona. You can experience different kinds of massage in this city. You can try the famous chocolate massage. This will allow you to experience what it feels like to get covered in chocolate! You can try the sea shell massage, too.

Address:Carrer de Mallorca, 180
Phone:+34 930 00 91 65
Website
http://kbcenters.com/
Map
https://goo.gl/maps/8uQhqqdW9B22

### (9)Go on a Treasure Hunt

You can go on a treasure hunt while you are in Barcelona. This fun activity will allow you to explore the winding streets of Barri Gotic. If you win, you get a bottle of Spanish wine as a prize.

Address:Plaça dels Pirineus, 3-4
Phone:+34 932 80 92 74
info@bcn-adventure.com
Website
http://www.bcn-adventure.com/en/
teambuilding/city-treasure-hunt.php
Map
https://goo.gl/maps/3DGRfr23T8C2

## (10)Explore the Beautiful Park Guell

The Park Guell is a magical spot that is great for picnic. You could find various tourist attractions inside the park. You can find municipal garden inside the park. You can also find the Gaudi's beautiful mosaic salamander called "El Drac".

Here are some of the things that you should see while visiting the

Park Guell:
- The Viaduct
- The Pavilion
- The Colonaded Pathway
- The Ceiling Mosaic in Hypostyle Room
- The Bird Nests

Phone:+34 902 20 03 02
Website
http://www.parkguell.cat/
Park Guell Map
https://goo.gl/maps/4NNxwYKRf3Q2

## (11)Enjoy the Magic Fountain Show

This is a "must see" Barcelona attraction. You will never see a fountain like the Font Magica Fountain. This fountain was built in 1929. Around 2 million tourists visit this fountain every year.

Address:Plaça de Carles Buïgas, 1
Magic Fountain Map
https://goo.gl/maps/ZrK383JPT6J2

## (12) Enjoy the Camp Nou Experience and FC Barcelona Museum

There is nothing like watching the Barca play a home match. But, you should also visit the FC Barcelona Museum. Camp Nou also has the largest Nike stores in the world. You can also buy affordable FCB scarves and T-shirts at stalls outside the stadium during match days.

Address:C. Aristides Maillol, 12
Phone:+34 902 18 99 00

Website
https://www.fcbarcelona.com
/tour/buy-tickets
Camp Nou Map
https://goo.gl/maps/6LmftNyVJKP2

## (13)Discover unique and fantastic modernist buildings

You will discover many beautiful and awe-inspiring modernist buildings in Barcelona. When you are in Barcelona, you should go and see these buildings:

### Casa Amatler

Address:Passeig de Gràcia, 41
Phone:+34 932 16 01 75
Website
http://www.amatller.org/
Casa Amatler Map
https://goo.gl/maps/b3HGG8exMWK2

### Casa Mila

Address:Provença, 261-265
Phone:+34 902 20 21 38
Website
https://www.lapedrera.com/ca/home
Casa Mila Map
https://goo.gl/maps/pbdty3Up8Vr

### Casa Batillo

Address:Passeig de Gràcia, 43
Phone:+34 932 16 03 06
Website
https://www.casabatllo.es/
Casa Batillo Map

https://goo.gl/maps/5Q5bhuFPYk72

Casa Batillo is one of the most beautiful buildings in Spain. It was designed by the great Antoni Gaudi. In fact, it is one of his masterpieces. It is located at the heart of Barcelona.

Casa Mila is also a fascinating modernist building. It is also known as La Pedrera. It was designed by Josep Maria Jujol and Antoni Gaudi.

Casa Amatler is a unique, modernist building designed by Josep Puig Cadafalch. The design is a mix of Catalan and Flemish style.

## (14) Tour inside the Sagrada Familia

There is nothing like the Sagrada Familia. It is one of the most unique and most recognized structures in the world. This magnificent church was constructed 1882 and it was designed by the world famous architect Antoni Gaudi.

You would be amazed by the remarkable geometric details. The church organ will also amaze you! It has 1,492 pipes!

Here are some of the architectural gems and monuments that you should see when touring inside this holy church:

- Nativity façade
- Nave ceiling
- The Sacred Family Cathedral
- The Glory Façade
- Museu Gaudi
- Apse
- The stained glasses
- The RosaryChapel
- The Passion Façade

Whether you are a devout Catholic or not, you will definitely enjoy the tour inside this magnificent church.

Address:Carrer de Mallorca, 401
Phone:+34 932 08 04 14
Website
http://www.sagradafamilia.org/
Sagrada Familia Map
https://goo.gl/maps/VPQ2dhdLz2N2

## (15) Climb the Montjuic Hill
Climbing the Montjuic Hil will provide an awesome and unforgettable experience. You will find the Palau Nacional, the Magic Fountain, and the Mies van der Rohe Pavilion.

The Monthuic hill is also the home of the Anella Olimpica or the Olympic Ring. You can find the various sports facilities that are specially built for the 1992 Olympics.

If you are a nature lover, you will truly appreciate the beauty of the Montjuic gardens. You will be amazed by the beauty of the Montjuic botanical garden called Nou Jardi Botanic. If you are a cactus lover, you should also visit the Jardins de Mossen Costa I Llobera.

The oldest structure in the Montjuic hill is the Castell de Montjuic. It was originally built as a fortress to protect Barcelona from its enemies.

Montjuic Hill Map
https://goo.gl/maps/LtkL1Y2godD2

### (16) Explore the mountain of Tibidabo

You could enjoy the beauty of Barcelona by climbing the mountain of Tibidabo. You could find the beautiful Sagrat Cor Church on top of this mountain.

You can also take a ride in the famous Red Aeroplane. This is a single carousel that will allow you to enjoy the view of the city.

Tibidabo was featured in the movie Vicky Cristina Barcelona. Tibidabo has a beautiful, scenic view that will take your breath away.

Barcelona is an wonderful city that you should visit during your lifetime. You could visit museums that highlight the city's rich culture, charming tourist spots, and do memorable things that you could not do anywhere else in the world.

Tibidabo Map
https://goo.gl/maps/8wj2z7KLNzR2

# 25

# LISBON INTRODUCTION

I want to thank you for downloading my book!!

Here's a quick overview of what this book offers:
-Learn about the city's rich history
-Find out the best way to get around the city
-Learn safety tips when touring Lisbon
-Figure out the different neighborhoods and their unique charac-
teristics
-Understand the best time to visit the city
-Explore the city's rich history through remarkable artifacts in their
best museums
-Discover Portuguese art in Lisbon's best galleries
-Find out where the best coffee and pastries are served in Lisbon

-Know where to go for late night party
-Stay on budget with the top 5 affordable Lisbon hotels
-Have a unique gastronomic experience at the Lisbon's top restau-
rants

-Build memories of a lifetime by trying out something special you can only do in Lisbon

Plus, we give you a head start at planning your trip with our sample 3-day itinerary!

Thanks again for downloading this book, I hope you enjoy it!

# 26

# A Brief History of Lisbon

## *UMA BREVE HISTÓRIA*
### A Brief History of Lisbon

Lisbon has survived through the ups and downs from amassing immense riches to suffering plagues, fires, revolutions, earthquakes, coups and dictatorship. Today, Lisbon stands strong as a beautiful city attracting many visitors from the world over, admiring its unique characteristics.

### The rich history of the through the ages
### From the Ancient Years

Many believe that Ulysses was the first one to land in Lisbon on his way home from the Trojan War. Its ancient name, Ulissipo or Olissipo means "enchanted port." The sure thing is that the Phoenicians settled here around 3,000 years ago. The Phoenicians gave it the name, Alis Ubbo which means "delightful shore." After the Phoenicians, the Greeks, Carthaginians and Romans eventually realized what a delight this place was.

Even then, Lisbon witnessed tribal chaos. The North African Moors emerged victorious. They ruled the land in 714. The Moors called it Lissabona. In an effort to defend the city from the Christians, the Moors put up fortifications. They continued to defend the city for 400 years.

In 1147 however, Christian fighters led by Dom Alfonso Henriques took over the city. In 1260, Alfonso III chose Lisbon as the capital because of its strategic central location and reliable ports.

When Vasco de Gama discovered a sea route to India, Lisbon became more productive. It rose as an opulent center for a vast empire. The city continued to soar in the 1800s after the discovery of gold in Brazil. Merchants came to Lisbon to trade jewels, silks, spices and gold.

Along with the growth of trade, architecture flourished during this era. It spoke of extravagance. Among the masterpieces built during this period include Manueline works like Belém's Mosteiro dos Jerónimos.

### Earthquake Shook Lisbon
Everything was going so well until November 1, 1755 when three

devastating earthquakes hit the city. The tremors created destructive tsunami and started fires all over Lisbon. 90,000 souls out of 270,000 were lost. The city was in ruins. There was a big question whether Lisbon will be able to regain it's former glorious status. Marquês de Pombal, the chief minister of Dom João I took charge of rebuilding the city. The goal was to create a simple and easy to manage style which is now very much visible.

### Chaos Continued to Plague Lisbon
Just as the city was getting back on its feet, Lisbon fell into a series of chaos. Napoleon and his forces took over the city in November 1807. They held Lisbon hostage for four years.

After Napoleon, the Republican movement grew stronger. In 1908, it became more turbulent when Dom Carlos and his son were assassinated in Lisbon at the Praça do Comércio. For the next 16 years, the city went under 45 changes in government. Lisbon witnessed another major assassination in 1918. President Sidónio Pais was killed at the Rossio station.

### Second World War
In the Second World War, Lisbon played a neutral role. However, a great number of spies went to the city.

In 1926 and 1974, coups shook the order in the city. In 1974 and the following year, refugees from the former African colonies flooded the city. It added to Lisbon's cultural diversity.

### Lisbon Getting Back on Its Feet

In 1986, Portugal came to join the European Community. It proved to be an excellent move. With the help of funds sent by the European Community, development restarted in the city. It was a much-needed help after fire destroyed Chiado in 1988. Facilities were improved and the streets were cleaned.

Lisbon was back on track. In fact, the city started hosting major events including the 1994 European City of Culture, the 1998 Expo and the 2004 European Football Championships.

In 2006, the city continued to bloom. Many development projects around the city were started and completed. This includes the restoration and reopening of the Praça de Touros or Lisbon's bullring. The metro system was improved, and an Alfama building rehab began construction.

After all the challenges, Lisbon has not lost its delightful charm. Many visitors from around the world flock the city to experience all that this beautiful city has to offer.

# 27

# Transport and Safety in Lisbon

*VIAJE COM SEGURANÇA*

**Getting Into Lisbon**

If you are flying into Lisbon, you will arrive at Lisbon Portela Airport.Getting into the city is easy using one of the transport options.Click the Airport link for transport into Lisbon.

Phone:+351 21 841 3500
Lisbon International Airport Website
http://goo.gl/duWMGN
Lisbon International Airport Map
https://goo.gl/maps/XdBzgdSnznm

## Transport and Safety in Lisbon

The streets of Lisbon are quite busy, which results to heavy traffic. Unless you are exploring farther districts like the Belém, you are better off wandering about the city center on foot. In case you need wheels to get you where you want to go, you can depend on the following means of transportation around Lisbon.

### City Trasport by By CARRIS

This is the operator for Lisbon's trains, subways, funiculars and buses. Tourist tickets can be bought from CARRIS booths, network train stations and Metro stations. A 1-day pass costs 3.70€. Bring your passport as it is a requirement for buying a tourist ticket.

CARRIS Website
http://carris.transporteslisboa.pt/en/home/

## By Metro

The large M signs stand for Metro. Single tickets are sold for 0.80€ while a 1 day pass will cost you 3.70€. The Metro is likely to be crowded on bullfight days. A lot of people take the transport to get to Campo Pequeno from Avenida da República. Transport is open from 6:30am to 1am.

An interesting thing about Lisbon Metro is the impressive art collection on display. When you get the chance to take the transport, do not miss lineup of sculptures, glazed tiles and paintings. You will see here some of the contemporary art work of famous and renowned Portuguese artists like Maria Helena Vieira da Silva and Maria Keil. You'll get to see fine art works on display at the following Metro stations: Marquês de Pombal, Campo Grande, Baixa/Chiado and Cais do Sodré.

Metro Website

http://www.metrolisboa.pt/

**By Bus or Tram**

These are the cheapest forms of public transport in the city. The steep way up to the Bairro Alto can be accessed through the eléctricos or trams. Lisbon also has double-decker buses as seen in the streets of London. Basic fare is at 1.40€. These public transportations run from 6am to 1am.

If the Metro has an impressive fine art collection, there are also antediluvian eléctricos which resemble the cable cars of San Francisco. They are no longer just a means of transport. The antediluvian eléctricos have become quite famous as a tourist attraction too.

Bus or Tram Website
http://carris.transporteslisboa.pt/en/home/

## By Train
If you want to go from Lisbon to another village or town, it is best to take the electric train. It has a single class of seat. The tickets are affordable and generally comfortable. From Lisbon, hop in from the waterfront Cais do Sodré Station. 1 way ticket costs 1.80€ to 4€ depending on where you are heading.

Cais do Sodré Station Map
https://goo.gl/maps/nG8tMvPuhKJ2

## By Funiculars
There are three funiculars in Lisbon: the Glória, the Bica and the Lavra. Glória runs from Praça dos Restauradores to Rua São Pedro de Alcântara. Bica takes the Calçada do Combro to Rua da Boavista route. Lavra can take you from east of Avenida da Liberdade to the Campo Mártires da Pátria. A one-way ticket costs 1.40€.

## By Ferry
Taking the ferry is wise if you want to avoid the heavy traffic. You

will also be treated with a scenic view. If you're heading to Cacilhas, take the boat from either Praça do Comércio or Cais do Sodré. You will be dropped off at the Estação do Barreiro from which you can take a train to head to Algarve or Costa Azul.

Ferries run throughout the day every 15 to 20 minutes. Travel time is around 15 minutes. A trip from Lisbon to Cacilhas costs 0.81€.

Praça do Comércio Map
https://goo.gl/maps/2JPGv45Tnyy
Cais do Sodré Map
https://goo.gl/maps/TtdyoCtR9nE2

## By Taxi

As compared to other major cities, Lisbon taxi fare is not as expensive which makes it a popular means of transportation in the city. The basic fare starts at 2.50€ which will take you as far as 153m. An additional 0.10€ is added to the basic fare for every 162m travelled. There will be a 20 percent additional if you're taking the taxi between 10pm and 6am. If you're carrying luggage that weighs over 66 pounds, the driver is allowed to charge you additional 50 percent. The standard tip is 20 percent.

## By Car

Lisbon is congested. That said, it is not wise to rent and drive a car if you're going around the city. Car rentals are only advisable if you're taking a trip out of town.

## Is Lisbon Safe for Tourists?

Lisbon is generally safe for tourists but just like other major cities, pickpockets and petty crimes are unavoidable. Be careful, especially around crowded areas like train and tram stations. Take usual precautions like wearing money belt to protect your belongings. You have to watch out for hash sellers too. Best of all, you should use your common sense. Don't do anything that you would not think about doing at home, in your own city.

Bring a good city map with you and familiarize yourself with the neighborhoods so you have lesser chances of getting lost. It's good to learn a few Portuguese words. If you can't then don't worry about it. You are likely to find locals who speak English willing to lend a helping hand.

Obtain visitor information from the tourist office located at the Palácio da Foz. The office is open from 9am to 8pm. You can also buy a Lisbon card here so you can avail of free city transportation. The Lisbon card also includes admission to museums and other city attractions. It can also be used to avail of discounts to events.

Palácio da Foz Map
https://goo.gl/maps/sJK18GvuZrF2
**(Emergency Number – 112)**

The Lisbon 1-day pass for adults costs 16€, 27€ for a 2-day pass and 34€ for a 3-day pass. Children between 5 and 11 years old can get a 1-day pass for 9.50€, 14€ for 2-day pass and 17€ for 3-day pass.

You can contact the main tourist office at phone number, 21/12-05-050.

# 28

# Areas of Lisbon

## Areas of Lisbon

Here are the major areas in Lisbon and must-see places in each neighborhood.

### Baixa

Lisbon's business district boasts of its buildings structured according to the Pombaline-style architecture, the simplistic and easy to manage style after the earthquake destroyed the city. The area houses Portuguese banks. The area includes the clothing stores at Rua Augusta. This is where you will find the goldsmiths and silversmiths at Rua Áurea and Rua da Prata respectively.

Baixa Map
https://goo.gl/maps/PqqucK5wWDB2

## Chiado
The west of Baixa leads to this neighborhood known as Lisbon's shopping district. The finest shops in Lisbon like the famous porcelain and china store, Vista Alegre is found here. A Brasileira, the coffee shop where Portuguese literati gather is also located in this area.

Chiado Map
https://goo.gl/maps/vRC7aoimoxm

## Bairro Alto
If you continue the climb from Chiado, you will reach Bairro Alto which means "Upper City." It is best to get to this area through a trolley car. Many of the buildings here were untouched by the destructive that hit the city in 1755. Among the things you will find in this neighborhood are excellent restaurants, exciting bars and nightclubs as well as charming antique shops. You have to be careful threading the streets at night though, as addicts and drug dealers hang out here.

Bairro Alto Map
https://goo.gl/maps/sBKQeyitnEU2

## The Alfama
This is Lisbon's oldest district. It is also known as the Moorish section. Most of the structures here were saved from the earthquake. This neighborhood is home to fishwives or varinas, fishermen and stevedores.

Also found in this area is the Visigothic fortification which the Romans used which is known as the Castelo São Jorge or St. George's Castle. As you climb up Alfama, you will pass by a major landmark, the House of the Pointed Stones or Casa dos Bicos. It is a 16th century townhouse with diamond-shaped stones adorning its facade. Avoid wandering in this neighborhood at night. Some parts of Alfama are where muggers wait for unsuspecting victims.

The Alfama Map
https://goo.gl/maps/QD2Pyzyf2U32

## Belém

The suburban part of the city, Belém houses the Portugal's fine monuments that were built in the Age of Discovery. Before the 1755 earthquake, Belém used to be an aristocratic sector where elegant town houses abound.

Tourists flock the area for two reasons: Mosteiro dos Jerónimos and the Museu Nacional dos Coches. Mosteiro dos Jerónimos is a Manueline structure built in the 16th century. The Museu Nacional dos Coches or National Coach Museum is unique and considered the finest the world has ever seen. Regarded as the land of museums in the city, Belém also houses the Museu de Marinha and the Museu de Arte Popular.

Belém Map
https://goo.gl/maps/Gu1YdY3jhLM2

## Cacilhas

The neighborhood of the working class, Cacilhas also houses the best seafood restaurants in the city. It can be accessed through a ferry ride from the Praça do Comércio or through the Ponte do 25 de Abril. Constructed in 1966, this bridge stretches 2.2km long and towers at

190m height. Ponte do 25 de Abril has the longest suspension is all the bridges in Europe. Another notable structure in this neighborhood is the Ponte Vasco da Gama that makes the north of Portugal, southern Algarve, east of Alentejo and southern Spain more accessible.

Cacilhas Map
https://goo.gl/maps/YZZiHxQDTZx

## Uptown

Uptown Lisbon is both a residential and business district consisting of 20th century apartments and office buildings. It houses the Calouste Gulbenkian Museum, the Fronteira Palace and the Campo Pequeno. This is also where one of Europe's largest shopping malls is found, the Colombo along with the post-modern Amoreiras.

Uptown Map
https://goo.gl/maps/gkHDTXdT7Ak

# 29

# Best Time To Visit

Lisbon has a nice location, seated in southeast Europe. This means the city enjoys hot summers with cool wind coming from the Atlantic. The winters are mild here too. The average temperature in July and August is at 79.3°F. The temperate winter averages at 60°F. Rain, however, falls heavily between November and March. That means Lisbon is good to visit for most parts of the year. The city does not run out of reasons to celebrate throughout the year with an impressive list of events.

The city of Lisbon greets the year with a series of festivals. The list includes Lisbon Fish & Flavours. The gastronomic festival is a delight for foodies. Classes and demonstrations are also held in the Commerce Square during the event.

By April, Lisbon holds a Book Fair at the Edward VII Park where colorful stalls are set up. But the biggest event of the year by far is the Festas de Lisboa of June where the streets of the city center and the Alfama are greeted by a barrage of music, parties, parades and dances.

In August, the city prepares for the Jazz em Agosto. The event pays tribute to jazz music. Live bands play at the Calouste Gulbenkian Foundation. In November, Arte de Lisbon is held at the Nation's Park. By year end, Lisbon holds a series of New Year's Eve concerts and exciting firework displays at the Commerce Square.

Now you can schedule your trip according to the event you'd like to see in Lisbon.

# 30

# Lisbon's Best Museums

*VAMOS EXPLORAR A HISTÓRIA*

**Lisbon's Best Museums**

One of the top reasons why visitors from all over the world come to Lisbon is the exquisite line-up of museums. Lisbon's rich history is depicted in various art forms. If you want to learn more about Lisbon's amazing story, you better check out at least one of these museums.

## Calouste Gulbenkian Museum

This great museum in Lisbon carries one of the finest art collections in all of Europe. On display are more than 6,000 art pieces that were accumulated for more than 4,000 years. Some of these paintings date back to antiquity. These art pieces were once owned by Calouste Gulbekian, an Armenian oil magnate, who donated his estate to the nation. The museum dedicated to this man was inaugurated in 1960.

You should allot at least 2 hours to go through these valuable artifacts. Among the must-sees are the Roman medallions which were found in Egypt, Thomas Germain's crafted silverware, Turner's The Wreck of a Transport Ship, Armenian illustrated manuscripts from the 16th century and the Noveau jewelry by Lalique.

To get to this museum, take the Metro to either São Sebastião or Praça de Espanha Stations.

Address: Avenida de Berna, 45A, Uptown Lisbon
Phone: +351 217 823 000
Opening Hours: Wed-Mon, 10am-6pm
Calouste Gulbenkian Museum Website
http://gulbenkian.pt/museu/Museu/en/Homepage
Calouste Gulbenkian Museum Map
https://goo.gl/maps/ZoDfVp3v94U2

## Museu do Oriente

Portugal has forged cultural links with the Orient. The artifacts displayed in this museum are proof of that. The highlights include the 17th-century Namban screen which depicts the arrival of Portuguese explorers in Japan and the intricate teak door from India. This door is said to date back to the 18th century. It has beautiful bronze and iron trimmings too. Another special feature of the museum is an exceptional piece from Macau. It is a child's cradle in the shape of a boat. There are also exquisite silver alloy bracelets from East Timor.

Address: Doca de Alcantara, Lisbon, 1350-352
Phone: +351 21 358 5200
Opening Hours: Fri (10am-10pm), Tue-Thu, Sat-Sun (10am-8pm)
Museu do Oriente Website
http://www.museudooriente.pt/?lang=en
Museu do Oriente Map
https://goo.gl/maps/39hh35xvg6z

## Museu Nacional do Azulejo

This museum is dedicated to decorative tiles or what the Portuguese call, azulejo. Located in the historical Convento da Madre de Deus from 1509, Museu Nacional do Azulejo's tiles are displayed in a chronological order.

The exhibit starts with the early 16th century Moorish tiles with multi-colored design. One of the highlights is the Nossa Senhora daVida altar piece which showcases the development of Portugal's own style of tile making. There's another interesting piece, a 35-metre tiled panorama representing Lisbon before it was ruined by the 1755 earthquake. It is known as Portugal's longest azulejo. Admission to the museum includes entry to the Madre de Deus church.

Address: Rua da Madre de Deus,4 Lisbon, 1900-312
Phone: +351 21 810 0340
Opening Hours: Tue-Sun (10am-6pm)
Museu Nacional do Azulejo Website
http://www.museudoazulejo.pt/en-GB/default.aspx
Museu Nacional do Azulejo Map
https://goo.gl/maps/TavXXASzNHC2

## Museu Escola de Artes Decorativas da Fundação

### Ricardo do Espírito Santo

Located in the Palácio Azurara, the museum has an impressive collection of paintings, textiles, ceramics, pieces of furniture, gold and silver from the 17th and 18th centuries. Do not miss the exquisite ornate rooms. The biggest highlight includes the 1510 tapestry woven in silk and wool, the ewer with King Manuel I's armillary sphere from the Ming Dynasty and the 18th century woolen carpet which comes from Arraiolos.

Address: Largo das Portas do Sol 2 Lisbon, 1100-564
Phone: +351 21 881 4600
Opening Hours: Wed-Mon (10am-5pm)
Museu Escola de Artes Website
http://www.fress.pt/
Museu Escola de Artes Map
https://goo.gl/maps/Y4UaPBbhtTU2

### MUDE — Museu do Design e da Moda

This interesting museum is located in what used to be a bank. Museu Design Moda has some of the most interesting designs and fashion classics. The exhibit focuses on vintage apparel. The works of haute couture designers from the 50s and 60s like Yves Saint Laurent and Coco Chanel are on display here. There are designs from Giorgio Armani, Paco Rabanne, Vivien Westwood and Mary Quant as well.

Interior designers like Ray Eames, Charles and Phillipe Starck are also well represented in the museum. There are a few surprises for visitors like a Piaggo classic Italian scooter. Everything in this museum is a fashion delight.

Address: Rua Augusta 24, Lisbon, 1100-053
Phone: +351 21 888 6117
Opening Hours: Tue-Sun (10am-6pm)

MUDE Website
http://www.mude.pt/?lang=en
MUDE Map
https://goo.gl/maps/kpTWqMtS9k82

## Museu de Marinha

Found in the Jerónimos monastery, this is one of the most engaging museums in Lisbon. The focus of the museum is maritime history and is dedicated to Portugal's seafaring tradition. The tour starts at the Discoveries Hall displaying intricate model ships. These displays showcase the development of ship building starting from the 15th century onwards.

Museu de Marinha also has a vast collection of astrolabe which is the biggest in the world. It includes a Willem Jansz Blaeu's terrestrial globe from 1645. You should watch out for the royal yacht of Amélia and its exquisite wood panel cabin constructed in 1900. There are plenty of maritime paraphernalia on display too like navigational instruments and charts. In the main building, you will find the Santa Cruz which is a seaplane used to cross the trans-south Atlantic in 1922.

Address: Praça do Império, Lisbon, 1400-206
Phone: +351 21 362 0019
Opening Hours: Daily (9am-5pm)
Museu de Marinha Website
http://ccm.marinha.pt/pt/museu
Museu de Marinha Map
https://goo.gl/maps/BAatD2kHJaN2

# 31

# The Best Art Galleries in the City

## The Best Art Galleries in the City

Because of Portugal's rich culture and history, artists can draw inspiration from many things. Lisbon prides itself as a patron of the arts. Many galleries have been established to support artists of the past and the present. If you like art and curious to see what Portuguese artists come up with, do drop by at least one of these amazing galleries.

### Museu Nacional de Arte Antiga
This is the country's national gallery. Its vast collection of Portuguese paintings from the 15th and 16th centuries is the largest in Portugal. It also features stunning European paintings from the middle ages up to the 19th century. In addition to paintings, Museu Nacional de Arte Antiga also has an extensive display of applied art; most of which are from the Discover age and Exploration era.

A 17th century palace houses the museum. The highlights include the Nuno Gonçalves' exquisite Panels of St Vincent from 1470 and Hieronymus Bosch's The Temptations of St Anthony.

Address: Rua das Janelas Verdes 9, Lisbon, 1249-017
Phone: +351 21 391 2800
Opening Hours: Wed-Sun (10am-6pm), Tue (2pm-6pm)
Museu Nacional de Arte Antiga Website
http://www.museudearteantiga.pt/english
Museu Nacional de Arte Antiga Map
https://goo.gl/maps/XjquQojUaBq

### Alecrim 50 Galeria de Arte
A newly opened art gallery, Alecrim 50 Galeria de Arte was established in 2006 and is located in Chiado. The main goal of the gallery is to promote the works of artists while they are still in their career's early stages. They put on display art works that demonstrate innovation, unquestionable talent and superior creativity. The art works on display vary from paintings to photography, sculptures to installation art.

Address: 50 Rua Alecrim, Lisbon, Portugal
Phone: +351 21 346 5258

Opening Hours: Tue–Sat (2pm–7pm)
Alecrim 50 Galeria de Arte Website
http://www.alecrim50.pt/
Alecrim 50 Galeria de Arte Map
https://goo.gl/maps/mgnYEuJeyXP2

### Centro de Arte Moderna

Established in 1983, this art gallery showcases art collection from the 20th to 21st century. Centro de Arte Moderna also sets up temporary exhibits featuring the works of homegrown talents and international artists. Its permanent collection consists of 9,000 pieces focused on Portuguese art. Among those on display are the works of Antonio Dacosta, a Portuguese painter that spearheaded the surrealist movement in the country. There are magnificent works from Amadeo de Souza Cardoso as well, the forefather of modernism in Portugal. Drawings, paintings and objects from the Portuguese visual storyteller, Paula Rego.

Address: Rua Dr Nicolau de Bettencourt, Lisbon
Phone: +351 21 782 3474
Opening Hours: Wed–Mon (10am–6pm)
Centro de Arte Moderna Website
http://gulbenkian.pt/cam/
Centro de Arte Moderna Map
https://goo.gl/maps/kuYD7DaNVLS2

### São Mamede Galeria de Arte

Established in the 60s, this art gallery promotes the works of Por-tuguese contemporary artists. The highlights include the Alexandre Manuel's incomparable black and white photography, António Areal's surrealist sketches and paintings along with Rui Matos' modern sculptures. While it dedicates itself to Portuguese art, São Mamede Galeria de Arte also holds exhibit for international artists like the works of Shintaro Nakaoka, a renowned Japanese sculptor.

Address: 167 Rua da Escola Politénica, Lisbon
Phone: +351 21 397 3255
Opening Hours: Mon-Fri (11am-8pm), Sat (11am-7pm)
São Mamede Galeria de Arte Website
http://www.saomamede.com/
São Mamede Galeria de Arte Map
https://goo.gl/maps/QHoa5pq9j1T2

# 32

# Best Coffee Shops in Lisbon

### *AMO CAFÉ*

### Best Coffee Shops in Lisbon

Did you know that the Portuguese spend most of their money and time hanging out in cafés? They surely love to drink coffee and eat some pastries. Coffee shops are an institution in Lisbon. They do not only serve excellent coffee. They also provide an enticing atmosphere with some of the most picturesque views.

If you want coffee, ask for bica or espresso. In this city, strong bica is always paired with a light meal. Aside from their coffee though, you should also try their milky galão or latte and pasteis de nata or custard tarts.

### Cruzes Credo Café

After a long walk in Alfama, there's no better way to rest than a seat in a lovely cafe with good customer service and nice music. This is exactly what you get from Cruzes Credo Café. It's a favorite among locals because of their excellent coffee and mouthwatering food.

Do try their burgers and toasts along with their irresistible chocolate cake and gourmet toasts. Their burgers are best enjoyed with natural juice or beer, while the coffee and chocolate cake is a match made in heaven.

Address: Cruzes da Sé, 29, 1100 Lisboa
Phone:+351 21 882 2296
Opening Hours: Daily, 10am-2pm
Cruzes Credo Café Website
https://www.facebook.com/cruzescredo/
Cruzes Credo Café Map
https://goo.gl/maps/MRUy9rUVmoo

### Cafe Versailles

If you're heading uptown, you might as well stop by at Cafe Versailles, turn-of-the-century Lisbon café that serves coffee, hot chocolate and sweet pastry. The interior is designed Baroque style adorned with stained glass, engraved mirrors, carved wooden panels and crystal chandeliers. The grand space is quite inviting. Unlike other cafés in the city, the place is less crowded by tourists but locals love it even if they have to take the metro to get here. Why? Locals say Cafe Versailles has the best pastries in all of Lisbon.

Address: Avenida da Republica, 15a, Uptown Lisbon
Phone: 21 354 6340
Opening Hours: Daily (7:30am–10:00pm)
Cafe Versailles
https://goo.gl/2BirNa
Cafe Versailles
https://goo.gl/maps/PApW41brZ1P2

### Café Nicola

This is one of the most popular cafés in Lisbon not just because of its excellent location overlooking the Rossio square. Café Nicola has plenty to offer. For one, it is a historical café where the literary artists from the late 19th century would meet up. The lovely interior is furnished with Art Deco and polished marble adorned with outstanding canvases inspired by Manuel Barbosa du Bocage, a Portuguese poet from the 18th century. Its European café society atmosphere is quite the scene.

The café also has an excellent outdoor terrace where guests can enjoy a spectacular view while sipping their fantastic coffee. The coffee is nothing less than perfection, imported from the world's premier coffee producers, Sao Tome e Principe in South Africa and Brazil. Aside from their great tasting coffee, Café Nicola also serves delicious breakfast.

Address: Praça Dom Pedro IV 24–26 Lisbon
Phone: +351 21 346 0579
Opening Hours: Mon-Fri (8am–10pm) Sat (9am–10pm) Sun (10am–7pm)

Café Nicola Website
https://goo.gl/9iSIYs
Café Nicola Map
https://goo.gl/maps/XSUdtJYiSPz

## A Brasileira

Lisboans like to meet up at this café before they go to the theatre or see a performance. A Brasileira is more than a hundred years old. The greatest Portuguese poet, Fernando Pessoa, used to hang out here. Journalists, artists and writers back in the day also liked to meet here. When you see this place, you'll be charmed by its lovely interior with the old carved wood and metal décor furnishings. Find a seat outside in the charming terrace and listen to the songs of musicians as they pass by the streets of Chiado.

Address: Rua Garret, 120-122 Lisbon
Phone: +351 213 469 541
Opening Hours: Mon-Sun (8am-2pm)
A Brasileira Website
https://goo.gl/7IUcuN
A Brasileira Map
https://goo.gl/maps/ijDzsaYdvvw

## Café Pastelaria Benard

This is another charming coffee shop but often ignored because it's close to Café A Brasileira.  If you are looking for an authentic experience however, without having to squeeze into a crowd, Bernard is the right place to be. It exudes a genuine 19th century atmosphere. Its pastries and cakes are absolutely delicious. The coffee is excellent as well.  But Bernard is most known for their chocolate croissants. The lovely terrace is quickly filled up especially in the warm summer months.  The locals love coming here for some afternoon tea and yummy sandwiches.

Address: Rua Garrett 104, Lisbon, 1200–205
Phone: +351 21 347 3133
Opening Hours: Daily (8am–11:30pm)
Café Pastelaria Benard Website
https://goo.gl/yuiR1e
Café Pastelaria Benard Map
https://goo.gl/maps/jthG7pa2FTB2

# 33

# Lisbon's Best Bars and Night Clubs

*A NOITE É UMA CRIANÇA*

### Lisbon's Best Bars and Night Clubs

If you want to chill after a long day of serious touring, you can do so in a cozy bar. Lisbon has plenty to offer. The city has an exciting nightlife and you are more than welcome to join the party!

### Clube da Esquina

Located in Bairro Alto, it's a favorite hangout spot not only because it is incredibly inexpensive but also because they serve the most interesting mixes, popular all over the city. Their concoctions include mojitos and caipirinhas but they are most famous for the morangoska.

The atmosphere is mellow and relaxed. It is the perfect place to chill along with the mixed crowd. The DJ plays jazzy-funk soundtracks but the bar also invites guest DJs.

Address: Rua Barroca 30-32, Lisbon
Opening Hours: Daily (7pm-3am)
Clube da Esquina Website
https://www.facebook.com/clubedaesquina.bairroalto
Clube da Esquina Map
https://goo.gl/maps/3AVapDW8dju

## Portas Largas

You will have no trouble finding this bar because everybody knows it. Portas Largas or "Large Doors" used to be a fado house. Although it has been transformed into a hip bar, its origin is still apparent. The azulejo panel was maintained along with the old furniture. The ad hoc appeal actually works.

Portas Largas is especially popular in the summer. After ordering a mojito or caipirinha, head outside to Rua da Atalaia and join the laid back crowd. The bar treats its guests with live music from Brazilian or African combo.

Address: Rua da Atalaia 105, Lisbon 1200-038
Opening Hours: Daily 8pm-4am
Portas Largas Website
https://goo.gl/jPq9xA
Portas Largas Map
https://goo.gl/maps/MuYmtgSxv1o

## Station

How cool is it to hang out in a club overlooking the river? You can do that in this funky waterfront Station. The coolest part about this nightclub is the superb sound system. They play a mix of disco-tech and soul. If you want to get inside the club, you have to make a little effort in dressing up. The crowd is fashionable and sophisticated yet the vibe is familiar. Station is especially popular within the glitzy social circuit of Lisbon.

Address: Cais do Gás, Armazém A, Lisbon 1200-109
Opening Hours: Thu-Sat 11pm-6am
Station Website
http://www.station-club.com/
Station Map

https://goo.gl/maps/jV91AhGMjZC2

## Cinco Lounge
Sophisticated and cool at the same time. That's the best way to describe Cinco Lounge, a bar run by people who manage Michelin-starred restaurants so you can trust that they know what they are doing. Everything is topnotch from the decor to the service.

It's a little pricey but it comes highly recommended. Try out their freshly original cocktail mixes. And don't miss out on the sushi and other good snacks.

Address: Rua Ruben A. Leitão, 17-A, Principe Real, Lisbon
Website: cincolounge.com
Cinco Lounge Website
https://www.facebook.com/CINCO.lounge/
Cinco Lounge Map
https://goo.gl/maps/KJPjzg45aP42

## Ministerium
Housed in what used to be Lisbon's Ministry of Finance, Ministerium prides itself with special 18th century architecture. The club takes advantage of its historic appleal. Its classic decor however, is a complete opposite to the modern music the DJs play who happens to be the savviest ones in Portugal.

You can't help but dance to the cool techno-electronica soundtrack. If you're in the city on a Saturday, you're in luck. Ministerium as a nightclub only opens on Saturday nights so make sure to check out this hip Lisbon club.

Address: Terreiro do Paço, Lisbon 1100-038
Opening Hours: Sat (11pm-6am)

Ministerium Website
https://www.facebook.com/MinisteriumClub/
Ministerium Map
https://goo.gl/maps/B5tnsdBbuVN2

# 34

# Top 5 Affordable Hotels

## Top 5 Affordable Hotels

You don't have to spend loads of cash to avail of comfortable accommodation. You just need to find the top rated but affordable hotels in the city. To help you out, here are the top five hotel recommendations.

### Hotel Borges

Located in Lisbon's most fashionable neighborhood, Chiado, Hotel Borges offers an elegant accommodation at a friendly starting rate of 42.00€ per person per night. The 3-star hotel treats you to a stunning view of Tagus River. It's close to several major attractions including the Museum of Contemporary Art, San Carlos theatres and Chiado Museum.

With close to a hundred rooms available, you can choose from a single to double to triple rooms. Every room gives access to modern amenities. You can even request a room with a balcony for better viewing of the surrounding areas.

Address: Rua Garret Nº108 Baixa, Lisbon
Phone: +44 (0) 2071004522
Hotel Borges Website
http://www.hotelborges.com/hotel-overview.html
Hotel Borges Map
https://goo.gl/maps/4zjP29pFZMp

### Browns Downtown Hotel

This 3-star has been awarded the Certificate of Excellence winner by TripAdvisor. Browns Downtown Hotel feels like home providing you with all the modern comforts you are used to and more. It is conveniently located near taxi services, train stations and bus stations so guests can get around the city much easier. Plus, it's close to the Tagus River, the Comercio Square and St. George's Castle.

Address: Rua dos Sapateiros, 73 - Lisbon
Phone:+351 213 431 391
Browns Downtown Hotel Website

http://www.brownsdowntown.com/
Browns Downtown Hotel Map
https://goo.gl/maps/6EFUGCvZJB82

### Eduardo VII Hotel

This charming 3-star hotel is a wonderful place to stay at with its interesting design reminiscent of the past centuries. While the interior has an old world feel, Eduardo VII hotel does not fall short in providing modern amenities. A big bonus is the hotel is only a few minute walk to the Baixa Chiado area, the Parque Eduardo VII and the Marques de Pombal Square. The room rate starts at 44.02€ per person per night

Address: Av Fontes Pereira de Melo,5 - Lisbon
Eduardo VII Hotel Website
http://goo.gl/kPI1NE
Eduardo VII Hotel Map
https://goo.gl/maps/EPZpsfR4Ksw

### Hotel Roma

Found in one of Lisbon's main avenues, Avenida de Roma, the 3-star Hotel Roma has an ideal location sandwiched between the commercial and residential area. From the hotel, you can easily access the city center. It is also close to the Bairro Alto and Chiado.

The hotel has 263 rooms with single, double, triple and quad rooms available. The rooms are well-equipped with modern facilities and amenities. The best part is the rates are affordable starting from 26.06€ per person per night.

Address: Av. de Roma, 33, Lisbon
Phone: +44 (0) 2071004522
Hotel Roma Website

http://www.hotelroma.pt/
Hotel Roma Map
https://goo.gl/maps/wdnUygUPTFu

### Hotel Dom Afonso Henriques

Hotel DAH is ideally situated for tourists to explore magnificent Lisbon. From the hotel, you can reach the city center in less than 10 minutes. It is also close to the airport. Local buses can be easily accessed from this accommodation and so are other means of transport.

The 2-star hotel is small with 39 rooms available but it provides quality accommodation at a great price complete in amenities. The room rates start at 28.00€ per person per night. Request a room with a beautiful view of the city and the stunning Tagus River.

Address: Rua Cristóvão Falcão nº 8, Lisbon
Phone: +44 (0) 2071004522
Hotel Dom Afonso Henriques Website
http://www.hoteldah.com/en
Hotel Dom Afonso Henriques Map
https://goo.gl/maps/6kT9m3JufFL2

# 35

# Top 5 Restaurants

## ONDE COMER

### Top 5 Restaurants

The food in Lisbon is just as exquisite as the sights. There's a mix of luxury and budget restaurants in the city. In this list, you will find places where you can get the most value for your money.

## Chicken All Around

If you like chicken then this is a must-try restaurant. This mid-range priced restaurant has a made a name reinventing chicken dishes. As you would guess, the star ingredient in all of the dishes is chicken and the main aim is to expound on chicken dish choices.

Among the menu highlights is the grilled chicken club sandwich served with exciting sauces like the spicy tandoori. It also comes with a Mexican fajita with crunchy salad garnishing. They also serve American barbecue and Jamaican or Thai style chicken. For dessert, order the chunky cheesecake or the crème brûlée de laranja.

Address: Mercado da Ribeira, Lisbon
Phone: +351 21 244 980
Chicken All Around Map
https://goo.gl/maps/fzU6hmk4VNp

## IBO Marisqueira

The focus of this restaurant is seafood. IBO Marisqueira serves seafood in all colors, shapes and sizes. Unique with a Mozambican heritage, the restaurant serves traditional recipes which are cooked to perfection. Their seafood platters are not only plated beautifully. They are also served in generous portions.

The menu highlights include the tiger prawns and the variety of shellfish. They have crab, lobster, oyster, mussel and cockle among many others. You will also find meat dishes. To complete your dining experience, try the Laurentina which is the Mozambican national beer.

Address: Rua Cintura do Porto 22 Lisbon
Phone: +351 929 308 068
IBO Marisqueira Website

http://www.ibo-restaurante.pt/
IBO Marisqueira Map
https://goo.gl/maps/QzWUfnBwGeR2

### Tascardoso

A casual restaurant in Bairro Alto, Tascardoso specializes in serving unpretentious traditional Portuguese cuisine. They have an interesting menu offering a variety of regional dishes. Among their most unique and must-try offering is the corvine which is a croaker fish steak grilled perfectly. Another unusual dish is the cuttlefish that's grilled in its own ink. They call is chocos assados com tinta. Tascardoso has a limited but excellent wine list.

Address: Rua de O Século 242-4, Lisbon 1200-439
Phone: +351 21 342 7578
Tascardoso Website
https://goo.gl/rs8E1s
Tascardoso Map
https://goo.gl/maps/mjj9Du9jqqw

### O Pitéu da Graça

You will rarely read about this unassuming and homely restaurant in travel guides but it is one of the best kept secrets of Lisbon. As a matter of fact, top chefs in Lisbon come here to eat.

The family-owned restaurant serves traditional Portuguese recipes which were handed down from generation to generation. They serve marinated and spiced Minho-style roast pork as well as turbot fillet served with pepper rice and tomato. Their plates are colorful and the dishes are absolutely flavorful. You can get here through the tram no. 28.

Address: Largo da Graça 95, Lisbon 1170-165

Phone: +351 21 887 1067

Opening Hours:   Mon-Fri (12nn-3pm) (7pm-10:30pm) Sat (12nn-3pm)

O Pitéu da Graça Map

https://goo.gl/maps/aqKD2L3kexn


## Feitoria Restaurante & Wine Bar

Aside from Chef Joao Rodrigues' Michelin-star menu, this Lisbon restaurant in Belem is sought after because of its great venue. Set by the waterfront, Feitoria Restaurante & Wine Bar provides diners with a compelling view of the Targus River.

The chef serves inventive traditional Spanish, Southern European and Portuguse dishes plated beautifully. The superb dining experience starts off with a hot or cold starter.  For the entree, you would want to try the sautéed Algarve scarlet shrimp with fresh cucumber garnishing. And for the main course, the smoked salami is exemplary. The succulent grouper with green peas is like no other.  Another highlight from the world class menu is the tender veal loin served with wild mushrooms. The restaurant also has an excellent and extensive wine list. Do try something you haven't tasted from home.

Dining at Feitoria Restaurante & Wine Bar is a little more expensive than others in this list. However, it is worth the try. Expect nothing less than an exciting gastronomic adventure from chef Joao Rodrigues and his team.  You would want to book a seat in advance.  If you're looking for a unique dining experience, order the creative menu but do so at least 2 days in advance.

Address: Altis Belém Hotel & Spa, Lisbon, 1400-038

Phone: +351 21 040 0200

Opening Hours: Mon-Sat (7:30pm-11pm)

Feitoria Restaurante & Wine Bar Website

http://www.restaurantefeitoria.com/en/
Feitoria Restaurante & Wine Bar Map
https://goo.gl/maps/cVyBMUUg78J2

# 36

# Special Things You Can ONLY DO in Lisbon

**EXPERIÊNCIAS ÚNICAS EM LISBOA**
Special Things You Can ONLY DO in Lisbon

What make a city special are the unique things you can experience from it. Do try these things while you're in the charming capital of

Portugal.

### Check out Campo Pequeno

Located in Uptown Lisbon, Campo Pequeno is a monumental building according to Moorish style. Constructed in 1892, the building features cupolas atop the main towers with a bullring that can accommodate 9,000 spectators.

Today, the bullring is used for bullfighting on Thursdays in season. It is also occasionally used for circus, concerts and other shows. Within Campo Pequeno, you will find cinemas, restaurants and a shopping mall too. To get here, take the Metro going to Campo Pequeno Station.

Address: Centro Comercial do Campo Pequeno,
1000-082 Lisbon
Phone:+351 21 073 0746

Campo Pequeno Bullring Map
https://goo.gl/maps/cg7LCjqMCEt

## Take the Antediluvian Eléctrico No. 28 to See the Historical Areas of Lisbon.

There used to be horse-drawn trams but in 1903 they were replaced by the eléctricos. This ride will take you to an interesting trip through the historical sites of Lisbon.

## Stop by at Casa dos Bicos

Dubbed as a 16th century architectural curiosity, Casa dos Bicos means "house of spikes." A total of 1125 diamond-shaped stones adorn its face. Many structures were destroyed by the earthquake but this palace stood strong. The arched windows are true to Portuguese Manueline style. It is only open during temporary exhibitions but even the view from the outside is spectacular.

Address:Rua dos Bacalhoeiros, 1100-135 Lisbon
Phone:+351 21 880 2040
Casa dos Bicos Map
https://goo.gl/maps/inPALJqa9MA2

## Sightseeing at Miradouro das Portas do Sol and Miradouro de Santa Luzia

These locations stand over the medieval and history-rich area of Lisbon. From here, you can gaze at the immense beauty of the city. Miradouro de Santa Luzia introduces you to Alfama. It greets visitors with a marvelous view overlooking the river, the beautiful churches and the medieval houses. At Miradouro das Portas do Sol, you will find St Vincent's statue with a boat in one arm and two ravens on the other. He is Lisbon's patron saint holding the city's symbols.

Miradouro das Portas do Sol Map
https://goo.gl/maps/cnsCPkdZEJ62
Miradouro de Santa Luzia Map
https://goo.gl/maps/jJdy7e2cw6T2

## Visit a 16th-century monument, the Sao Vicente de Fora Church.

Built in 1582 in honor of the crusaders and Portuguese soldiers who fought the Moors, the church was ruined during the earthquake but was restored in 1855. You can enter the church from the gate to the right. Admire the 18th century tiled panels that adorn its interior. The tiles depict some of the scenes from LaFontaine's Fables. You can also climb up to the roof and get a marvelous view of the Tagus River, the National Pantheon and the whole of Alfama.

Largo de São Vicente, 1100-572 Lisbon
Phone:+351 21 882 4400
Sao Vicente de Fora Church Map
https://goo.gl/maps/WVBkkyLAeWH2

### Explore Saint George's Castle.

This massive and millennium old structure is visible from nearly everywhere in Lisbon. Some sections that were built way back in the 6th century still stand. They were fortified by rulers from the Romans to the Visigoths to the Moors. It served as the residence of Moorish royals. When King Alfonso Henriques and the crusaders captured the walls, the castle was dedicated and named after England's patron saint, St. George.

Today, this historic castle is an oasis of peace and tranquility offering a picturesque view of the city. At the main gate, visitors are welcomed by the first king's statue along with cannons which is a constant reminder of the castle's initial purpose. You can climb up the towers for the views, stop by at the archeological museums in the underground chambers or relax in the beautiful gardens.

Explore the castle from March to October between 9am and 9pm, from November to February between 9am and 6pm.

Address:R. de Santa Cruz do Castelo,
1100-129 Lisbon
Phone:+351 21 880 0620
Saint George's Castle Website
http://castelodesaojorge.pt/en
Saint George's Castle Map
https://goo.gl/maps/HzXDvfViKn62

### Watch the sunset from Doca do Jardim do Tabaco.

This is one of Alfama's prided attractions. Its name means "Tobacco Garden Dock" as it used to be the city's main depot for tobacco. Jardim do Tabaco offers a stunning view of the sunset at the breathtaking Tagus River. Known as the trendiest waterfront, it has plenty of excellent restaurants with outdoor seating. There are trendy shops and nightclubs here too.

Address:Av. Infante Dom Henrique 34,
1100-280 Lisbon
Doca do Jardim do Tabaco Map
https://goo.gl/maps/rbGwHAKN1Jy

### Stop by at Fronteira Palace

Constructed in 1640, this beautiful residence located in the suburb of Benfica in Uptown Lisbon has stunning gardens, spectacular decorative tile work, oil paintings and frescoed panels. Tourists come here to walk along the formal gardens with tiles that depict religious scenes, battles and hunting. There are magnificent fountains, statues and busts of Portuguese kings too.

To book the guided tour in advance, you may call (+351) 21 778 2023. It is a private residence but you can join a guided tour to this lovely palace through the rooms and gardens. The guided tour occurs every 30 minutes from 10:30 to 12nn on Mondays to Saturdays.

Address:Largo São Domingos de Benfica 1,
1500-554 Lisboa
Phone:+351 21 778 2023
Fronteira Palace Website
http://www.fronteira-alorna.pt/
Fronteira Palace Map
https://goo.gl/maps/oAYfVwQ7UwA2

# 37

# 3-Day Itinerary

## A 3-Day Itinerary

## Day One

- 6:30am Breakfast at the Hotel
- 7:00am Take the antediluvian eléctrico no. 28 to Alfama
- 7:30am Enjoy the view at Miradouro de Santa Luzia and
- Explore Miradouro das Portas Do Sol
- 8:30am Walk to Sao Vicente de Fora Church for a quick peek
- 9:00am Visit Saint George's Castle
- 10:30am Explore the sights around the Comercio Square including the Casa dos Bicos
- Check out the tourist shops in the area as well
- 12:00pm Taste the traditional grilled fish dishes from restaurants nearby
- 1:30pm Visit the Decorative Arts Museum
- 3:30pm Visit Museu Nacional do Azulejo
- 6:00pm Watch the sunset from a café at Doca do Jardim do Tabaco
- 7:30pm Check out the trendy shops
- 9:30pm Dinner by the waterfront
- 11:00pm Check out Station nightclub

## Day Two

- 6:30am Breakfast at the Hotel
- 9:00am Check out one of the museums in Belém
- 11:00am Take a taxi to Fronteira Palace, Uptown for a guided tour
- 1:00pm Lunch
- 2:30pm Head to Calouste Gulbenkian Museum
- 4:30pm Visit Campo Pequeno
- 5:30pm Stop by at Amoreiras or Colombo, one of the largest shopping malls in Europe
- 7:00pm Have a quick bite at Cafe Versailles
- 9:00pm Dinner

## Day Three
- 6:30am Breakfast at the Hotel
- 8:00am Wander around Praça do Comércio
- 9:00am Check out the stores at Rua Augusta
- 11:00am Walk along Rossio
- 12:00nn Lunch at Café Nicola
- 1:30pm Praça dos Restauradores
- 2:30pm Estação do Rossio
- 3:00pm Visit Rua Áurea and Rua da Prata for the finest gold and silver
- 4:30pm Elevador de Santa Justa
- 5:30pm Stop for snacks
- 9:00pm Dinner at a restuarant of your choice
- 10:00pm Stop by at Clube da Esquina

# 38

# Conclusion

I want to thank you for reading this book! I sincerely hope that you received value from it!

If you received value from this book, I want to ask you for a favour. Would you be kind enough to leave a review for this book on Amazon?

**Check out my other books !!**

https://www.amazon.com/Florence-Short-Travel-Italy-Guides-ebook/dp/B017L5ZNLW/

https://www.amazon.com/Venice-Short-Travel-Guide-Guides-ebook/dp/B00ON3KZLE/

https://www.amazon.com/Copenhagen-Short-Travel-Denmark-

Guides-ebook/dp/B017WLXX3K/

https://www.amazon.com/Berlin-Short-Travel-Germany-Guides-ebook/dp/B013OODR1Q/

trademark owner. All trademarks and brands within this book are for clarifying purposes only and are the owned by the owners themselves, not affiliated with this document.

Made in the USA
Middletown, DE
15 January 2019